Mountain Biking Marin

40 Great Rides in Marin County

Theresa Martin and Brian Simon

Maps by Don Martin

Inquiries should be addressed to:
Martin Press
P.O. Box 2109
San Anselmo, CA 94979
email bike@marintrails.com
or visit our website at www.marintrails.com

ISBN 0-9617044-7-0

Printed in the United States of America

Photo Credits:
All photos by Don Martin except the following,
Pages 95 and 96: Photos © Rolling Dinosaur Archives

Cover Photo Location:
Lake Lagunitas

Foreword

Marin is unique in the Bay Area, indeed unique in the country, for its rich environmental treasures. No other county can boast 3 national parks, 6 state parks and more than 20 other open space and water district lands. From the coastal cliffs of Point Reyes National Seashore to the ridges and valleys of Marinwood Community Services District, an open trail is only a stones throw away for most residents.

Soft paths through shady conifer woodlands, and verdant moss-covered rocks can be found on Mt. Tamalpais. Historic ranches and grazing cattle dot the ridges and valleys of West Marin. Magnificent coastal ranges lie at the edge of our continent, and redwood forests form an intricate web of life with animals and shade-loving plants. This is the Marin that nature lovers treasure.

Mountain biking is a great way to see this natural Marin. When mountain biking pioneers like Joe Breeze made their inventions widely available, we gained a great form of transportation. On the bike, you can become one with the environment and revel in the freedom of the open trail. There is a trail for every type of rider in Marin, whether you love the camaraderie of the well-used arteries to the top of Tam, or a remote single track where your only company might be the solitary fox or a bevy of quail.

This is the Marin we invite you to explore. We have catalogued our favorite rides, and found new rides for you to explore. We hope you have great adventures! Please let us know what you think. Our web site is www.marintrails.com and you can email us at biking@marintrails.com.

We would like to thank everyone who helped provide information for this book, the rangers at China Camp State Park, members of the organizations - Bicycle Trails Council of Marin and WOMBATS, our riding friends, and those we met on the trail, who stopped to provide good advice. We would especially like to thank Joe Breeze for providing the history section, Wende Cragg for the historical photos, Greg Martin and Kellar Autumn for critical advice and Katie Martin for her professional editing. The errors and mistakes that remain are our responsibility.

We greatly appreciate all the work our publisher, Don Martin, did in creating the maps and guiding the book to completion. Without his support, this book could not have been written.

Theresa Martin and Brian Simon

Table of Contents

Ride Starting Points

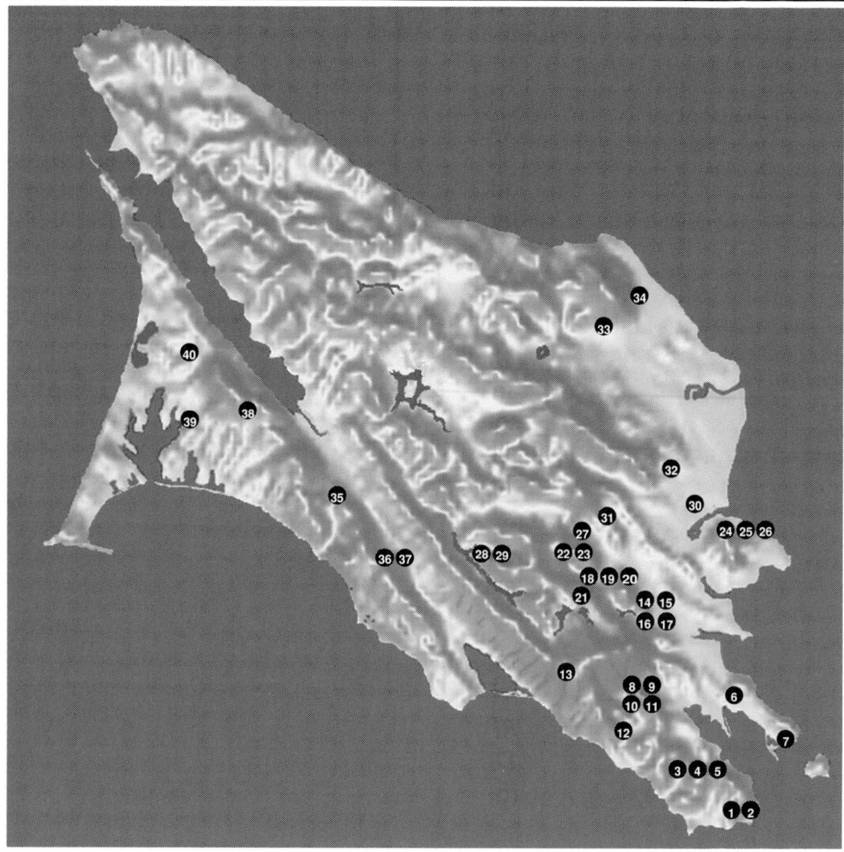

Southern Marin
Rides 1-5 start in Golden Gate National Recreation Area
Rides 6 & 8-11 start in Marin County Open Space
Ride 7 starts in Angel Island State Park
Rides 12-13 start in Mt. Tamalpais State Park

Central Marin
Rides 14-23 start in Marin County Open Space
Rides 24-26 start in China Camp State Park
Ride 27 starts in Marin County Open Space
Rides 28-29 start in Samuel P. Taylor State Park

North Marin
Ride 30 starts in Las Gallinas Sanitary District
Rides 31-34 start in Marin County Open Space

West Marin
Rides 35-40 start in Point Reyes National Seashore

How to Use This Guide

Welcome to Marin County, birthplace of mountain biking and home to miles of incredible trails in spectacular settings! We invite you to use this book to find new trails and explore different ride combinations. The book provides a wide range of rides, from simple, fun beginner rides, to long enduro rides, to tough, technical single track rides. Marin County offers rides for every ability, and this book provides a resource for those who want to get out and explore.

Choosing a Ride

There are three main factors to consider when choosing a ride. First, know your abilities and how they relate to our descriptions. If we describe a ride as moderate and you find it strenuous, then adjust your choices accordingly. Second, take the weather into consideration. Some south-facing fire roads like the Old Railroad Grade can get blazing hot in the summer. Third, read the trail descriptions carefully to choose and plan your rides.

The front of the book offers two helpful aids, a trip locator map showing ride starting points and a selection of best rides.

Trail Descriptions

Here is a sample entry of a trail description with a brief explanation.

Distance: 13.2 miles   ***Riding Time***: 2 hours
Elevation Change: 2300'   ***Difficulty***: Moderate
Technical Rating: 6   Fire roads with one technical single track.

Distance and Riding Time

Distance measurements refer to the total trip distance in miles. We have included the time it took us to complete the ride. We did not include time we took for breaks. When planning your ride, be sure you allow time for breaks, admiring views and enjoying the scenery. We consider ourselves to have good aerobic fitness, so that less fit riders might allot themselves more time.

Difficulty and Technical Ratings

The difficulty rating is a subjective measure of the fitness required.

Easy - Less than 10 miles total, less than 700' of climbing and not too steep. Good for families and inexperienced riders.

Moderate - Can be longer or steeper or both. Also may require some technical riding skill to handle the hills.

Strenuous - Long rides or steep climbs. These rides require strong aerobic fitness and because of steep hills, good technical skills.

We love technically challenging rides. Successfully climbing rocky trails, making steep ascents or descents is one of the great joys of riding. Our technical skill levels are as follows;

Skill 1-3 for beginners. Fairly smooth surface, hills not too steep.

Skill 4-7 for intermediates. Some ruts, roots or rocks possible. Moderately steep hills. Descents may require shifting weight back. Be able to pick a line and follow it with good balance. Can stay in control on moderate downhill or stop when required.

Skill 8-10 for advanced riders. Able to handle rough surfaces, tight turns and steep downhills.

Elevation Change

Elevation Change helps to determine how strenuous the ride is. A 1300' change means the ride climbs 1300' and descends 1300'.

Ride Directions/Using the Map

Each ride description includes mileage to key junctions with some junctions numbered. Numbered junctions, appearing like this ❶, also appear on the map and most numbered junctions appear on the elevation profile.

All trails or roads open to mountain bikes will be shown on the maps. However, not all hiking trails are shown. Note that some fire roads have names with "trail" in them, like Coastal Trail, which are shown.

Often used acronyms and abbreviations in the book include:

Acronym	*Meaning*
FR	fire road
FT	fire trail
MMWD	Marin Municipal Water District
GGNRA	Golden Gate National Recreation Area
MCOSD	Marin County Open Space District
Tam	Tamalpais
mi.	mile
yds.	yards

Using the Maps and Elevation Profiles

The trail maps show local roads, trailheads, water locations, elevation profiles and ride directions. Number labels correspond to key junctions indexed in the ride description on the left. The trail map is a 3-dimensional rendering of the area you're riding in. It is displayed so that no part of the map is any closer to the observer than any other part. Scales shown on the map are approximate for three reasons;

elevations have been exaggerated, small twists and turns in the road are not shown and the maps are viewed at a camera angle of 25°, which exaggerates the front of hills and diminishes the back of hills.

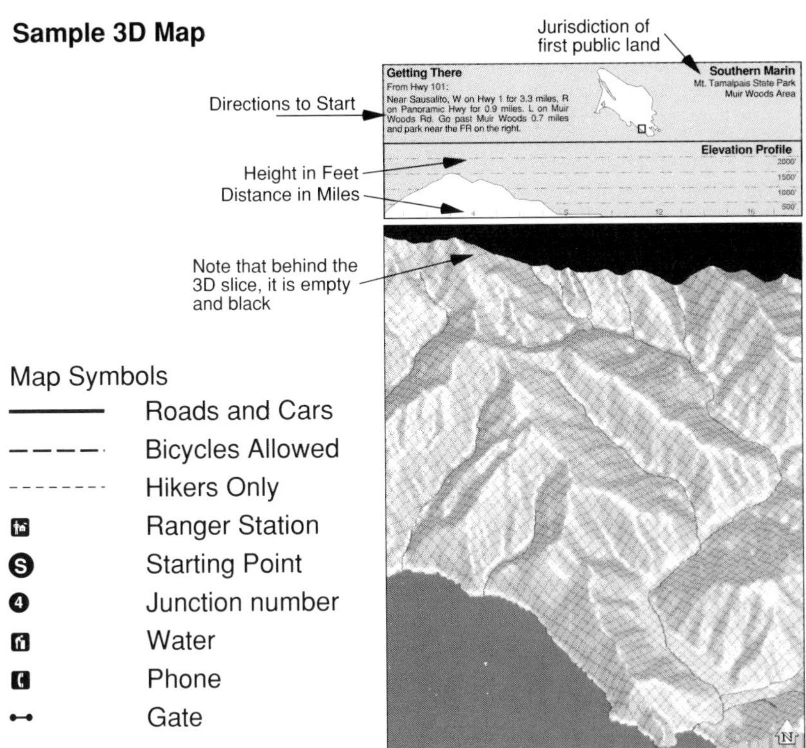

Suggestions and Precautions

As mountain bike riding becomes more popular, it attracts a wide variety of people with different levels of riding ability. We offer the following suggestions and precautions, especially for beginning riders.

What to Take on a Ride

Some of the rides in this book, like those in open space lands, are short and often in full view of civilization. The only essential item to take is water. However, when riding in more remote areas, such as Mt. Tamalpais or Point Reyes, it is best to be prepared. Here is a sample check list of things to take: fluids, windbreaker, book or map, extra food, knife, flashlight, compass, first aid kit, helmet, suncreen, money, tools: spoke wrench, chain tool, screw driver, allen wrenches, box/open end wrenches, pliers, swiss army knife, patch kit, spare tube, pump, duct tape and whistle.

Riding Alone

Riding alone is not recommended. However, if you do go out alone, tell someone where you are going and when you will return or leave a note in your car at the trailhead with this information.

Fluids

Fluids are essential when riding or staying outdoors. Often, people go riding or go to the beach and wind up the day with a mild headache. Usually, this is attributed to too much exposure, too much sun or too much wind. Many times, the problem is too little fluids. Bike riding requires a minimum of 1/2 quart of fluid per hour, and often more, depending on the temperature and elevation change. Alcohol does not count. It is a diuretic which means that it removes fluid by osmosis in the stomach. It is always a good idea to carry water and to drink it whether you feel thirsty or not

Plan to drink at least 1/2 quart of fluid per hour on rides.

Poison Oak

Poison oak for some is a minor irritation, for most, a major irritation and for a few, a medical emergency. The best advice is to learn to identify the plant by its leaves and avoid touching it. An old saying is,

"Leaves of three, leave it be."

In fall, poison oak leaves turn crimson red and drop off. In winter, the bare branches are difficult to identify, yet still retain their toxic oils. It helps to stay on designated trails and to watch out for branches that lean out onto the trail or drape down over the path. Poison oak is very common in Marin County.

Poison Oak

Stinging nettles also cause skin irritation if touched. Usually, nettles are small and only hit the legs if you have shorts on. The sting will generally last from 2-8 hours. If you rub the sting with an alder leaf, it might relieve the symptoms.

Mountain Lions

If you do see a mountain lion, don't ride away. Stand your ground, keep eye contact, make yourself look bigger, perhaps using your jacket or pack. Then, slowly back away. If attacked, fight back.

Parking

When parking on narrow streets, please respect local neighborhoods. Most cities require a 12' pavement clearance for emergency vehicles.

Disclaimer - Don't Rely on This Book

When it comes to trail safety, there are three reasons why you can't rely on this book. First, trails change. Roads develop ruts, trees fall down, signs change and rides change. In winter, some trails and roads may be impassable. Second, to paraphrase an old saying from general semantics, "the map is not the trail." No matter how descriptive the map or text is, it can't describe each and every feature, root or rut. Third, the book contains errors, not on purpose, but there are errors just the same.

The only safe way to ride is for you to stay in control at all times. We can not accept responsibility for trail conditions or for trail information. This is our disclaimer that we do not accept liability or legal responsibility for any injuries, damage, loss of direction or time allegedly associated with using this book.

IMBA Rules of the Trail

Thousands of miles of dirt trails have been closed to mountain bicyclists. The irresponsible riding habits of a few riders have been a major factor. Do your part to maintain trail access by observing the following rules of the trail, formulated by IMBA, the International Mountain Bicycling Association. IMBA's mission is to promote environmentally sound and socially responsible mountain bicycling.

1. *Ride on Open Trails Only.* Respect trail and road closures (ask if not sure), avoid possible trespass on private land.

2. *Leave No Trace.* Practice low-impact cycling.

3. *Control Your Bicycle.* Obey all bicycle speed regulations.

4. *Always Yield Trail.* Make known your approach well in advance. A friendly greeting or bell is considerate. Anticipate other trail users around corners or in blind spots.

5. *Never Spook Animals.* All animals are startled by an unannounced approach, a sudden movement, or a loud noise. Give animals extra room and time to adjust to you. When passing horses use special care and follow directions from the horseback riders (ask if uncertain).

6. *Plan Ahead.* Know your equipment, your ability, and the area in which you are riding. Be self-sufficient, keep your equipment in good repair, carry necessary supplies, and wear a helmet.

If you have comments, contact IMBA at: P.O. Box 7578, Boulder, CO 80306-7578 USA. Tel: 303/545-9011.

A Selection of Best Rides

Best Rides with Single Track

5 Tennessee Valley - Diaz Ridge (11.5 mi.)
11 Old Railroad Grade to East Peak Loop (18.0 mi.)
18 Camp Tamarancho - White Hill Loop (12.5 mi.)
25 Bay View - Shoreline Trails at China Camp (10.3 mi.)
38 Inverness Ridge Loop (11.1 mi.)
39 Estero Trail to Drakes Head (9.2 mi.)

Peak Bag Rides (all have great Bay Area views)

2 GGB to Rodeo Valley and Hill 88 (15.8 mi.)
11 Old Railroad Grade to East Peak Loop (18.0 mi.)
14 Bald Hill Loop (5.8 mi.)
17 Eldridge Grade to East Peak Loop (17.7 mi.)
22 Pine Mountain Loop (13.4 mi.)
26 Bay Hills Trail - Ridge FR - Bay View Trail (11.5 mi.)
27 Loma Alta Peak Loop (6.0 mi.)
28 Ridge Trail to Mt. Barnabe (7.4 mi.)
32 Loma Verde - Big Rock Ridge Loop (11.7 mi.)
34 Mt. Burdell Loop (8.3 mi.)

Other Great View Rides

5 Tennessee Valley - Diaz Ridge (11.5 mi.)
7 Angel Island Double Loop (9.7 mi.)
20 Deer Park to Stinson Beach Super Loop (47.2 mi.)
29 Bolinas Ridge Loop (13.2 mi.)
38 Inverness Ridge Loop (11.1 mi.)

Advanced/Expert Rides

5 Tennessee Valley - Diaz Ridge (11.5 mi.)
11 Old Railroad Grade to East Peak Loop (18.0 mi.)
17 Eldridge Grade to East Peak Loop (17.7 mi.)
18 Camp Tamarancho - White Hill Loop (12.5 mi.)
19 Deer Park - Pine Mountain - Repack (11.0 mi.)
20 Deer Park to Stinson Beach Super Loop (47.2 mi.)
22 Pine Mountain Loop (13.4 mi.)
28 Ridge Trail to Mt. Barnabe (7.4 mi.)
32 Loma Verde - Big Rock Ridge Loop (11.7 mi.)

Best Beginner Rides

6 Exploring Ring Mountain (6.0 mi.)
7 Angel Island Double Loop (9.7 mi.)
9 Old Railroad Grade to West Point Inn (13.2 mi.)
15 Shaver Grade - Bullfrog Rd. (10.2 mi.)
21 Sky Oaks Ranger Station to Lake Lagunitas (8.1 mi.)
24 Shoreline Trail to China Camp Village (8.1 mi.)
30 Las Gallinas Ponds - McInnis Park (7.7 mi.)
35 Bear Valley Trail (6.2 mi.)

Best Rides to See Lakes and Water

5 Tennessee Valley - Diaz Ridge (11.5 mi.)
7 Angel Island Double Loop (9.7 mi.)
20 Deer Park to Stinson Beach Super Loop (47.2 mi.)
21 Sky Oaks Ranger Station to Lake Lagunitas (8.1 mi.)
36 Five Brooks to Wildcat Camp (13.0 mi.)
39 Estero Trail to Drakes Head (9.2 mi.)
40 Marshall Beach and Abbotts Lagoon (13.8 mi.)

Good Winter Rides

2 GG Bridge to Rodeo Valley and Hill 88 (15.8 mi.)
9 Old Railroad Grade to West Point Inn (13.2mi.)
11 Old Railroad Grade to East Peak Loop (18.0 mi.)
16 Eldridge Grade - Lake Lagunitas Loop (11.2 mi.)
17 Eldridge Grade to East Peak Loop (17.7 mi.)
29 Bolinas Ridge Loop (13.2 mi.)
35 Bear Valley Trail (6.2 mi.)
38 Inverness Ridge Loop (11.1 mi.)
40 Marshall Beach and Abbotts Lagoon (13.8 mi.)

A Biker's Vacation Paradise (7 can't miss rides for the tourist rider)

5 Tennessee Valley - Diaz Ridge (11.5 mi.)
7 Angel Island Double Loop (9.7 mi.)
17 Eldridge Grade to East Peak Loop (17.7 mi.)
18 Camp Tamarancho - White Hill Loop (12.5 mi.)
19 Deer Park - Pine Mountain - Repack (11.0 mi.)
26 Bay Hills - Ridge FR - Bay View Trail (11.5 mi.)
38 Inverness Ridge Loop (11.1 mi.)

1 GG Bridge to Tennessee Valley

Distance: 13.2 miles *Riding Time:* 2 hours
Elevation Change: 2300' *Difficulty:* Moderate
Technical Rating: 5 Fire roads with one technical single track.
Coastal grassland and chaparral dominate this ride. Views of SF Bay and the ocean emerge as you cross each rolling hill. Springtime brings vast fields of diverse wildflowers. Best when sunny.

0.0 Start at the parking lot at the northwest side of the bridge. Ride up Conzelman Rd. past the bunkers.

1.2 Junction ❶. Go right on McCullough Rd. for 20', then take the Coastal FR left through a gate and down into Rodeo Valley. Be sure to keep your head up so you can enjoy the ocean views.

2.8 Bunker Rd. Cross the road and ride through a dirt parking area. Then cross a small bridge and go left on the Rodeo Valley trail (FR).

3.3 Junction ❷ of Miwok trail and Bobcat trail. Head straight onto Miwok trail (FR) and in about 100 yds., go right to continue on Miwok trail. This trail winds up the hillside towards Wolf Ridge. There are great wildflowers along the bank of this FR in the springtime.

4.8 Junction ❸ with Old Springs trail. Go left onto this cool little single track that crosses several bridges over fragile marshy areas before dipping down into Tennessee Valley. The trail gets a little technical towards the bottom and then dumps out behind the stables. Ride through the stables.

6.1 Junction ❹ and Tennessee Valley parking lot. Just before reaching the main road, take the gated Marincello FR on the right and ride up the moderate grade. Great views ahead as you climb steadily towards Wolfback Ridge. This FR is part of the Bay Area Ridge trail.

7.6 Junction ❺ with Bobcat trail. Go left. The trail swoops down and back up along the ridge.

8.2 Double junction. Go right to continue on Bobcat trail. Early morning is the best time to spot bobcats. The FR dips along the north side of the Gerbode Valley. Open grass and wildflower fields cover the hillsides as you round the tight downhill corners.

10.4 Junction with Rodeo Valley trail. Go left to retrace your ride back to the bridge. At **10.9** miles, turn right off Rodeo Valley trail into parking area next to Bunker Rd. Cross Bunker Rd. to climb back up to the ridge on the Coastal trail and the starting point at **13.2** miles.

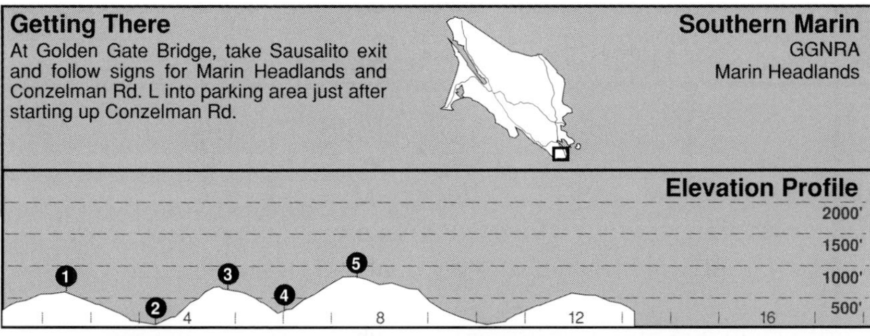

Hill 88
880'
Fort Cronkhite
Rodeo Lagoon
Marine Mammal Center
Tennessee Valley
Old Spring Trail
Miwok Trail
Marincello Trail
FAA Tower 1041'
Miwok Trail
Gerbode Valley
Oakwood Valley
Bobcat Trail
Bobcat Trail
Rodeo Drive
Bunker Road
Rodeo Valley Trail
Rodeo Valley
101
Slacker Hill 920'
SCA Trail
Conzelman Rd
5 minute tunnel Bikes OK
Waldo Tunnel
Sausalito
0 .7
Scale 1" = 0.7 miles

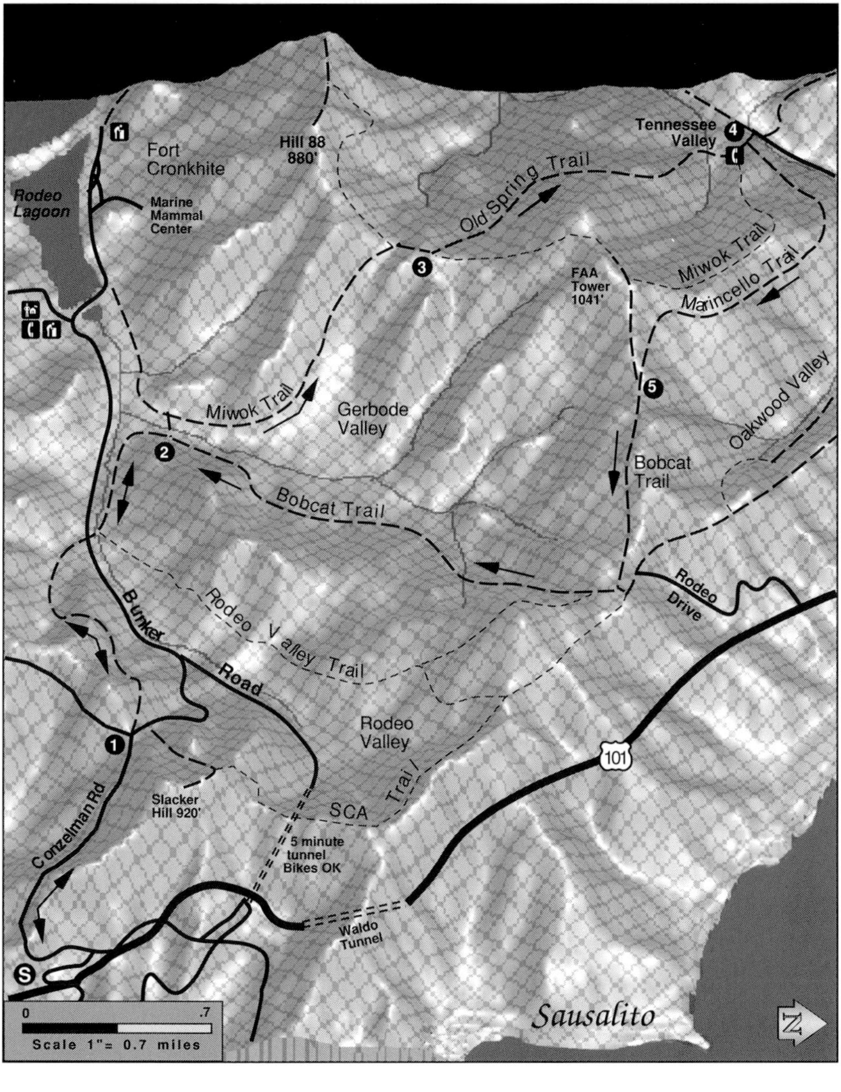

2 GG Bridge to Rodeo Beach and Hill 88

Distance: 15.8 miles *Riding Time:* 2-2.5 hours
Elevation Change: 2500' *Difficulty:* Moderate
Technical Rating: 3 Mostly well-maintained fire roads.
Coastside cliffs and beaches bring you up to Hill 88. The 360° views include the Golden Gate Bridge, East Bay hills and the ocean. A great exploration ride for visitors to Marin and SF. Some paved road.

0.0 Start at the parking lot at the northwest side of the Golden Gate Bridge. Ride up the paved road to the junction with McCullough Rd.

1.1 Junction ❶. Continue uphill on Conzelman Rd.

1.8 Bunkers, Hawk Hill and end of two-way road. Continue down the paved road for some fast steep descents, with an ocean view on the left and the Point Bonita lighthouse in front as a beacon.

3.7 Junction ❷. Go left here and bear left at each junction ahead until you come to Battery Mendell and the Bird Island Overlook.

4.8 Bird Island Overlook and awesome coastal views. Now backtrack.

5.9 Junction ❷. Go left, then right, down past the Nike missile site.

6.5 Junction. Take Bunker Rd. left towards the beach.

7.4 Rodeo Beach and junction ❸. Ride past the parking lot to the gate, then start a climb up the paved road. Follow the trail and bike signs all the way to Hill 88. Near the top, the road becomes a trail, which turns to stairs to detour around a massive land slide.

9.3 Hill 88 at 880'. This was once a Nike missile radar station. Now it is a group camp site. Great views in all directions. Turn back and zip back down the way you came. Ride out of the parking lot and past Rodeo Lagoon along Bunker Rd.

11.8 Junction. At the end of the lagoon, just before the bridge, take the Miwok trail to the left, the first real dirt section of the ride!

12.2 Junction ❹. Take the Rodeo Valley trail right, then right again.

Option: You can add 7.1 miles and another 1400' elevation change by taking the Miwok trail left to Tennessee Valley then back along the Bobcat trail. See Ride 1 for map and details.

13.0 Junction with Bunker Rd. Cross the road to catch a FR that is Coastal trail. Look for some great wildflowers in March and April.

14.7 Junction ❶. Take Conzelman Rd. to the left and downhill.

15.8 Back at the parking area. **Option:** For more riding, continue under the bridge to explore East Fort Baker.

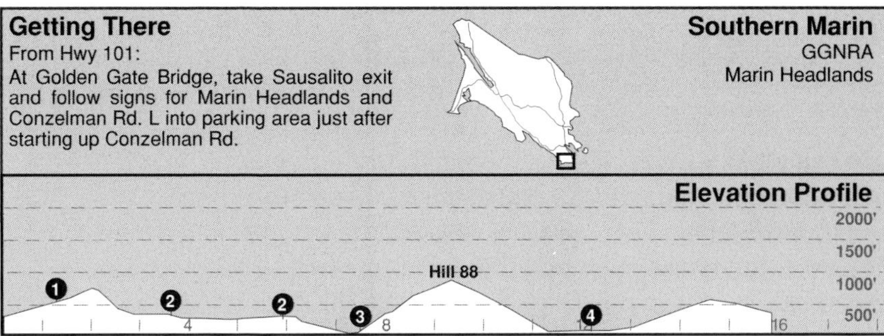

Getting There

From Hwy 101:

At Golden Gate Bridge, take Sausalito exit and follow signs for Marin Headlands and Conzelman Rd. L into parking area just after starting up Conzelman Rd.

Southern Marin

GGNRA
Marin Headlands

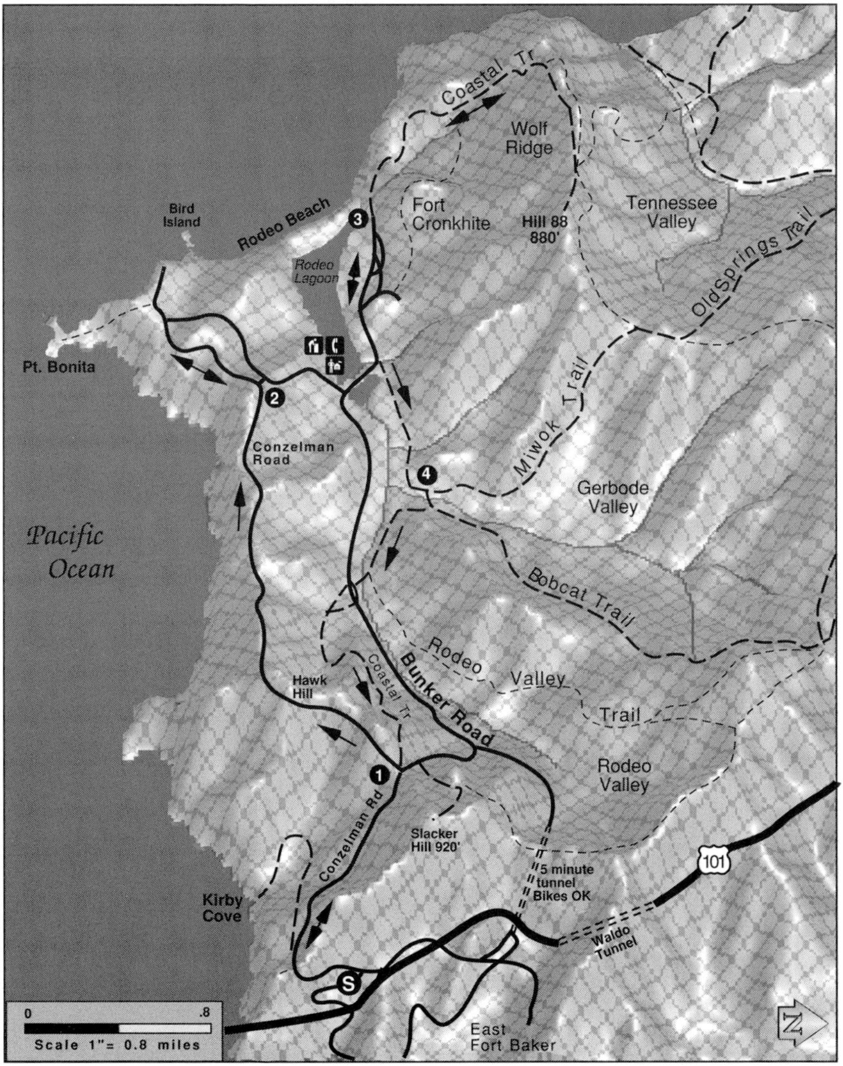

3 Coyote Ridge - Miwok Loop

Distance: 6.3 miles *Riding Time:* 1-1.5 hours
Elevation Change: 1200' *Difficulty:* Moderate
Technical Rating: 7 Tricky, single track descent.
A short, but challenging ride that heads down to Tennessee Cove, then climbs up Coyote Ridge for views of Mt. Tam and the ocean. The ride ends with a nice single track descent. Can be windy.

0.0 From the parking area take the main trail towards the ocean.

1.2 Junction ❶ with Coastal trail. Continue on the Tennessee Valley trail towards the beach.

View of Tennessee Cove

1.8 Beach and Tennessee Cove, which was named after the *S.S. Tennessee*, a side-paddle steamer that wrecked here in 1853 with 551 people bound for San Francisco and the gold rush. All survived. During certain times of the year, when the sand is lowered by wave action, it is possible to see remains of the Tennessee (parts of the engine) on the left side of the beach. When ready, backtrack to junction ❶.

2.4 Junction ❶. Take the Coastal trail left to begin the climb to the ridge. At the top of the hill, take the Coyote Ridge trail right uphill.

3.8 Junction ❷ with the Fox trail. Go left 100 yds. to a T-junction, then right to continue uphill on the Coyote Ridge trail. Great views.

4.0 Two junctions. Continue uphill past the two Green Gulch trails.

4.3 High point at 1031'. Near a wooden fence an unofficial spur trail leads left 30' to the rocky lookout and the highest point on this ride. A USGS plaque marks the spot. Great views in all directions.

4.4 Junction ❸. Go straight to take the Miwok trail, which heads towards a grove of eucalyptus trees.

5.1 Junction with FR to Marin Drive. At the bottom of a hill, in a grove of eucalyptus trees, head right. This area can be very muddy.

5.2 Junction ❹. Continue straight on the Miwok trail, which soon starts down a FR. The FR changes into a single track and gets steeper, with ruts and rubber waters bars - a good technical ride. Watch out for stairs at the switchbacks. Ride out to the parking area at **6.3** miles.

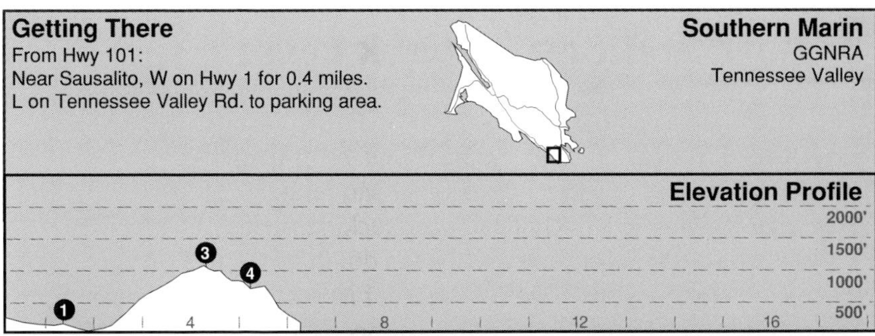

Getting There

From Hwy 101:
Near Sausalito, W on Hwy 1 for 0.4 miles.
L on Tennessee Valley Rd. to parking area.

Southern Marin
GGNRA
Tennessee Valley

Elevation Profile

2000'
1500'
1000'
500'
4
8
12
16

Muir Woods Rd
Miwok Trail
Diaz Ridge Trail
1031'
Miwok Trail
Green Gulch Farm
Coyote Ridge Trail
Middle Green Gulch
Haypress Camp
Tennessee Valley Rd
Fox Trail
Muir Beach
Coastal Trail
Coyote Ridge Trail
Pirates Cove
Coastal Trail
Valley
Trail
Tennessee
Coastal Trail
Hill 88
Tennessee Cove
0
.7
Scale 1"= 0.7 miles
N

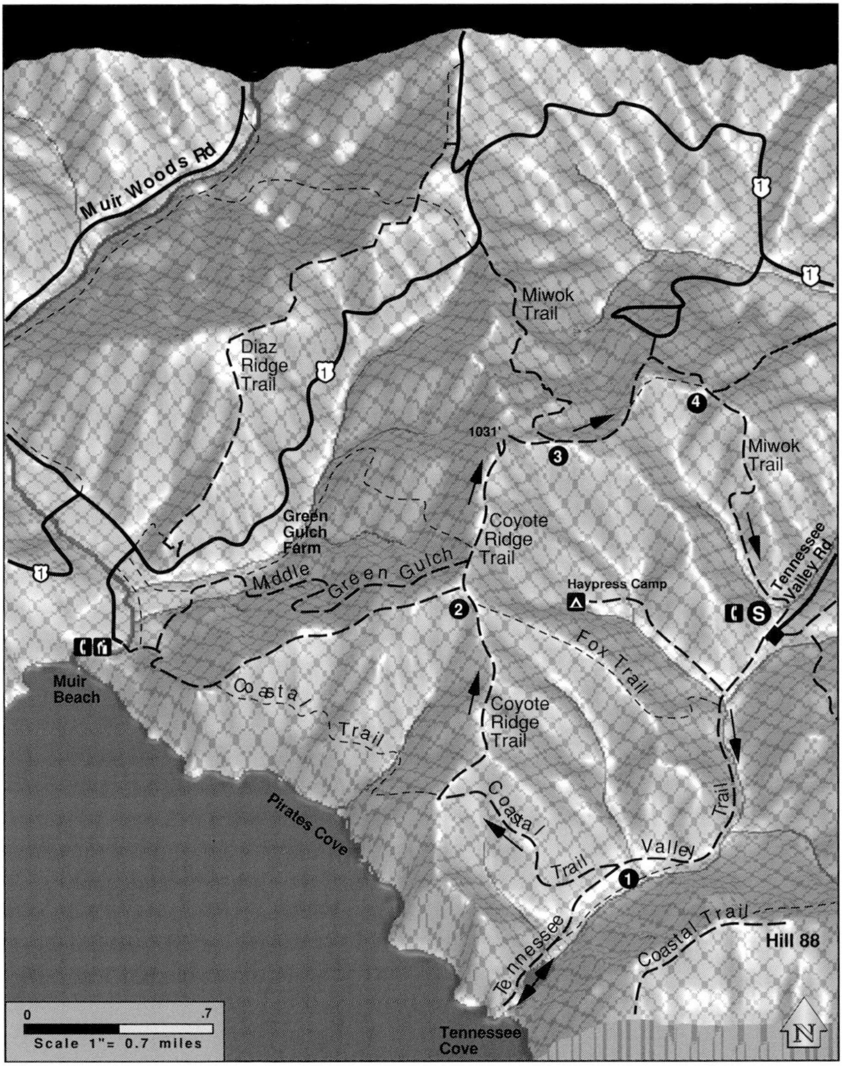

4 Marincello - Bobcat - Miwok Loop

Distance: 7.1 miles ***Riding Time:*** 1-1.5 hours
Elevation Change: 1400' ***Difficulty:*** Moderate
Technical Rating: 5 Some technical single track.
A beach to beach ride in rolling coastal grassland. Look for deer and bobcats in the early morning. Includes a fast single track descent. Best when spring wildflowers are present and/or when sunny.

0.0 Start at the parking area for Tennessee Valley. Ride towards the stables and take the Marincello trail (FR) that begins on the left about 50 yds. up the drive to the stables. The road climbs a moderate, smooth grade. This "trail" was once a 60' wide road that was part of the Marincello development, a proposed city of 30,000 slated for Gerbode Valley. The development was blocked in court for years and later, when the developer died, the land sold to the Nature Conservancy for $6.5 million. Later, it was given to the GGNRA.

There are nice views of Sausalito, Mill Valley and the bay as you're climbing. The Bay Area Ridge Trail includes this stretch of trail.

1.5 Junction ❶ with the Bobcat trail (800'). Go left as the trail swoops along the ridge that encircles the Gerbode Valley.

2.1 Junction ❷ with the Rodeo Valley trail and a connector trail. Take the Bobcat trail right and drop into the north side of the Gerbode Valley. In springtime look for wildflowers: lupine, poppies, brodiaea and iris. Also, keep an eye out for bobcat which have been sighted in the creek drainages along this road.

4.3 Junction ❸ with Rodeo Valley trail. Stay on Bobcat trail.

4.4 Junction with Miwok trail. Take a right and head back up the hill on the other side of the Gerbode Valley. The climb steepens towards the top. At **5.5** miles, Wolf Ridge trail heads west. Continue up.

Option: Go left down the Miwok trail to check out Rodeo Lagoon and the beach. If you want more hillwork, you can take the Coastal trail to Hill 88, adding a climb of about 1000'.

5.8 Junction ❹ with Old Springs Trail. Go left onto Old Springs. The trail is a wide, single track that crosses several wooden bridges over swampy areas and goes through a brief, rocky, technical section before dropping towards the back of the stables in Tennessee Valley.

7.1 Back at the parking lot.

Getting There

From Hwy 101:
Near Sausalito, W on Hwy 1 for 0.4 miles.
L on Tennessee Valley Rd. to parking area.

Southern Marin

GGNRA
Tennessee Valley

Elevation Profile

2000'
1500'
1000'
500'
1
2
3
4
4
8
12
16

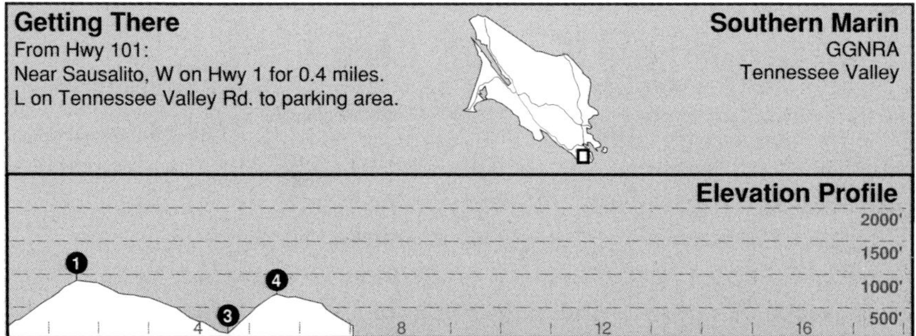

Tennessee Valley Rd
Marincello Trail
Oakwood Valley Tr
Alta Trail
101
Rodeo Ave Exit
Miwok Trail
S
Trail
Bobcat
1
2
Old Springs Trail
FAA Tower 1041'
Hawk Camp
Gerbode Valley
4
Trail
Miwok Trail
Hill 88 960'
Bobcat
3
Marine Mammel Center
Rodeo Valley Trail
Trail
Bunker Rd
Rodeo Lagoon
Coastal
0
.6
Scale 1" = 0.6 miles
N

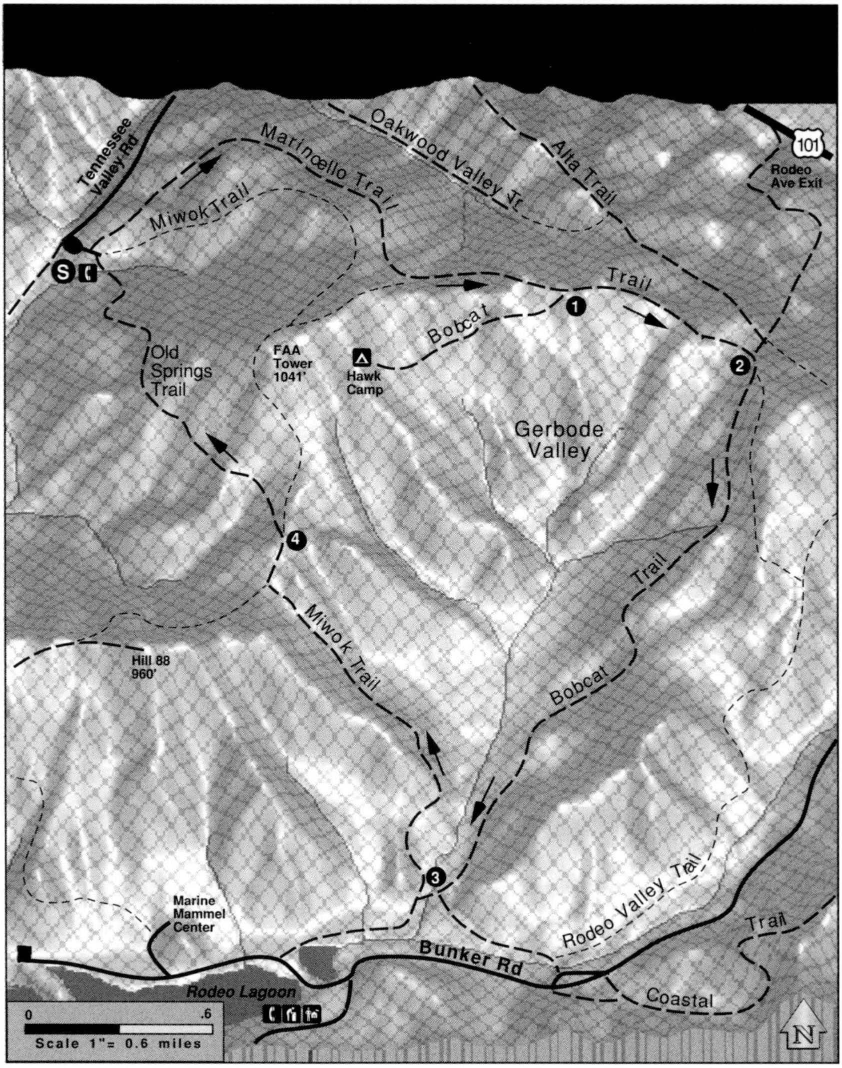

5 Tennessee Valley - Diaz Ridge

Distance: 11.5 miles ***Riding Time:*** 2-2.5 hours
Elevation Change: 2400' ***Difficulty:*** Moderate to strenuous
Technical Rating: 8 Technical single track climb and descent.
This is the best ride in the Marin Headlands for single track. A trip down Diaz Ridge to Muir Beach offers a spectacular view of the ocean. Best when clear and sunny. Muddy when wet. Can be windy.

0.0 Start at the parking area for Tennessee Valley. Ride back toward the exit of the parking lot and take Miwok trail on the left. The trail climbs up to a ridge, getting steep in sections. It also is rutted with water bars and stairs, a technical rider's delight.

1.1 Junction ❶ with FR. Go left. In about 80 yds., at a Y-junction, veer right to drop into a eucalyptus grove, muddy in winter. At **1.2** miles, another Y-junction. Go left and up along the Miwok FR.

1.9 Junction ❷ of Miwok and Coyote Ridge. Take Miwok to the right, an almost flat cruise with great views of Southern Marin.

3.4 Junction ❸ with Hwy 1. Go left along the highway for 100', then cross to continue on the Miwok trail.

3.8 Junction ❹. Take the Diaz Ridge trail left on a FR that rolls down along the ridge. It feels remote out here, untouched by civilization. Views to the ocean and Mt. Tam.

5.0 Junction. Go left through the gate. The trail is overgrown at first, then gets very steep and rutted in sections, as it drops towards Muir Beach. Views of the beach and surrounding hillsides. When you come to a Y-junction at a big rock, head left down to the highway.

6.1 Junction ❺ with Hwy 1. Go right for about 0.2 mile, then left past the Pelican Inn into the Muir Beach parking area.

6.6 Muir Beach. At the end of parking area, take the trail to the right over a creek, then turn left after crossing the bridge.

6.7 Go right onto Coastal trail. In about 200 yds., take the signed Middle Green Gulch trail to the left towards the Green Gulch Farm and Zen center. When you reach the fenced-in farm (**7.2** mi.), go left to cross the valley then right through a tall gate. Follow the Middle Green Gulch trail signs through another gate, then switchback up the hillside towards Coyote Ridge.

9.0 Junction ❻ of Coyote Ridge. Go left to pick up Miwok trail (**11.1** mi.) and return down the single track trail to the start at **11.5** miles.

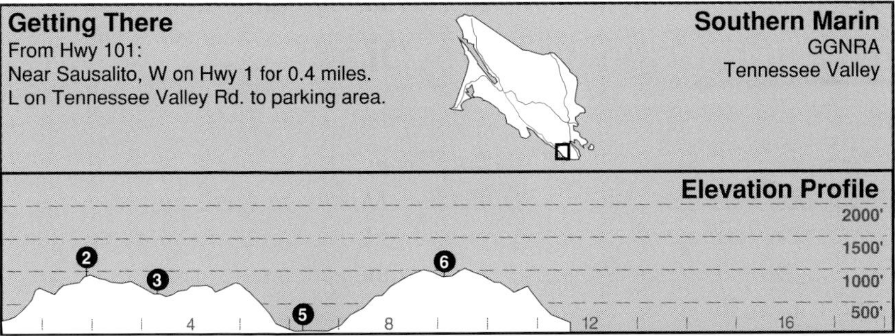

Getting There

From Hwy 101:
Near Sausalito, W on Hwy 1 for 0.4 miles.
L on Tennessee Valley Rd. to parking area.

Southern Marin
GGNRA
Tennessee Valley

Elevation Profile

2000'
1500'
1000'
500'
2
3
5
6
4
8
12
16

Muir Woods Rd
1
1
1
1
4
3
Miwok Trail
Diaz Ridge Trail
1031'
2
1
Miwok Trail
Coyote Ridge Trail
Green Gulch Farm
5
Middle
Green Gulch
6
Haypress Camp
Tennessee Valley Rd
S
Muir Beach
Coastal Trail
Fox Trail
Coyote Ridge Trail
Coastal Trail
Pirates Cove
Valley
Trail
Tennessee
Coastal Trail
Hill 88
0
.7
Scale 1"= 0.7 miles
Tennessee Cove
N

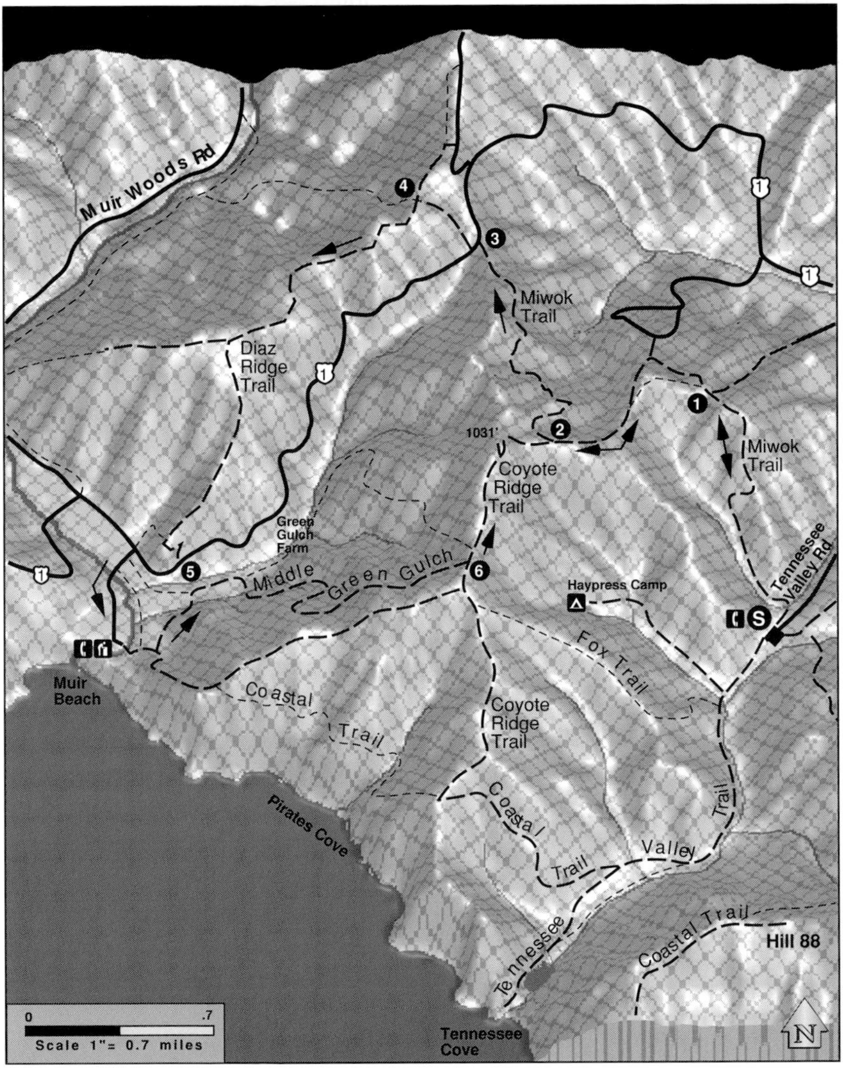

6 Exploring Ring Mountain

Distance: 6.0 miles ***Riding Time:*** 1 hour
Elevation Change: 850' ***Difficulty:*** Easy to moderate
Technical Rating: 4 Some eroded fire road. Some paved road.

Simple Indian petroglyphs and the rare Tiburon Mariposa Lily can be found near this peak on the Tiburon Peninsula. From March through May this is the best wildflower ride in Marin. Can be windy.

0.0 From Blackies Pasture and Richardson Bay Park, continue east on Tiburon Blvd for 100 yds. to the stoplight, then take Trestle Glen left.

0.6 Junction ❶. Go left on Shepherds Way for 100 yds., then right for 10' in towards the church parking lot. Look for the FR starting on the left. The road is very deeply eroded and moderately steep. In winter, it could be wet. You may have to walk a short section here.

1.2 Open space sign and junction. Continue straight uphill.

1.5 Junction ❷ and paved road. Ride past the water tank, then go right to the top of the mountain.

1.7 Ring Mtn at 602'. This big broad area was once a Nike radar site. Now it offers spectacular 360° views, and in spring, some great wildflowers. The most common flowers are gold fields and tidy tips. Both are yellow, but tidy tips are bigger and have white tips. After exploring the mountain top, head back on the paved road.

1.9 Junction ❷ again. Go straight.

2.0 Junction. Leave the paved road and take the dirt fire road left, heading straight towards Mt. Tam in the background.

2.3 Junction ❸ and saddle. There are two points of interest here. The large rock peeking over the hill on the left has some simple Indian petroglyphs on it. The Phyllis Ellman trail right leads down to a very rare, beige and yellow flower, the Tiburon Mariposa Lily. It is down the trail 300 yd., then left up the hill. It can be found in late May.

Continue up the steep rocky road to the top of the hill and a T-junction. Bear left. There are several spur roads and hiking trails leading off the main fire road. In general, this ride stays on the ridge as high and as long as possible.

3.9 Junction ❹ and fence just above the freeway. Head left downhill.

4.1 Junction. Take Central Drive to frontage road, then left to Tiburon Blvd. Go east to Greenwood Cove (**5.2** mi.), then take the bike route back to the parking area at **6.0** miles.

Getting There

From Hwy 101:

Near Mill Valley, E on Tiburon Blvd for 1.5 miles, R on Blackie's Pasture Rd. into Richardson Bay Park.

Southern Marin

Marin County Open Space

Ring Mountain

Elevation Profile

2000'

1500'

1000'

500'

1 2 4

4 8 12 16

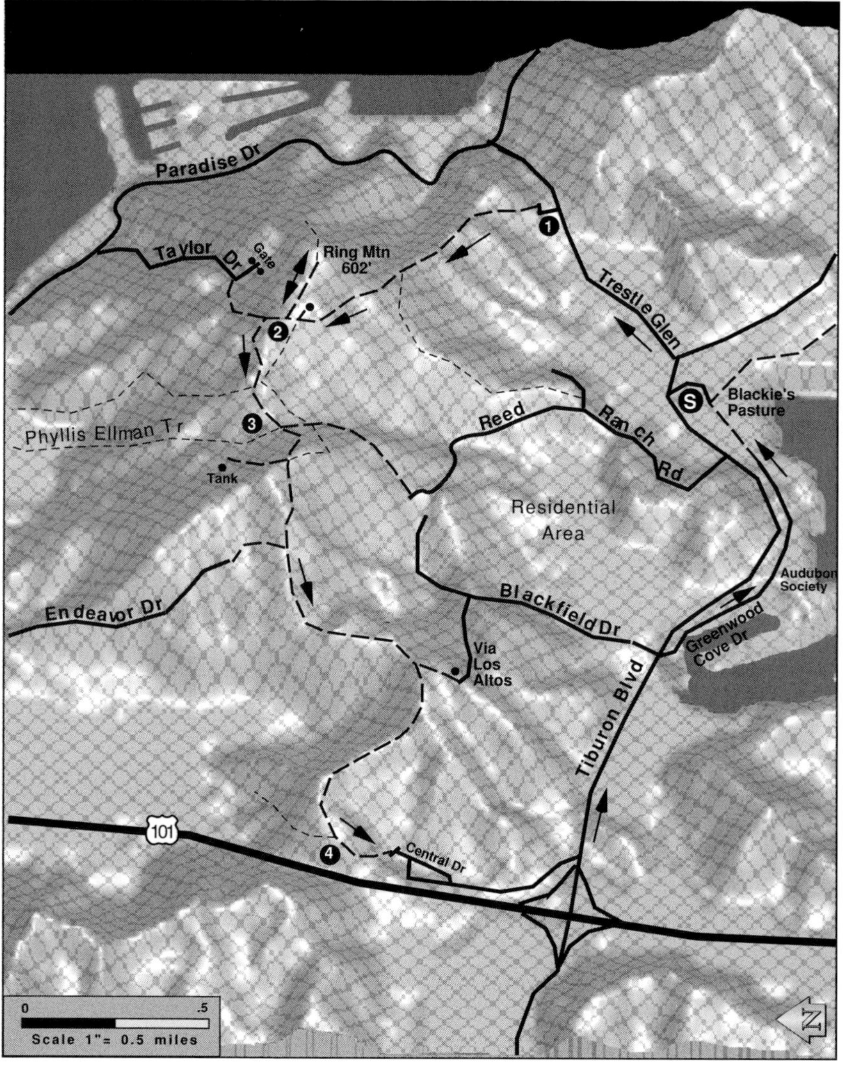

7 Angel Island Double Loop

Distance: 9.7 miles ***Riding Time:*** 1-1.5 hours
Elevation Change: 850' ***Difficulty:*** Easy to moderate
Technical Rating: 4 Some eroded fire road. Some paved road.
A ferry ride from Tiburon starts the bay area's only true island ride. A perfect ride to combine with a romantic picnic. The lower loop ride provides history and room to explore. Avoid when windy or foggy.

0.0 From the dock, go past the Visitor Center and museum at **0.2** mi. and take the bike trail left which switchbacks up to Perimeter Rd.

0.5 Junction ❶ with Perimeter Rd. Go straight from the trail to start your loop around the island in a counter-clockwise direction. Look for information plaques along the way that give historical context for the structures you see. At **1.3** miles, the road passes by West Garrison and Camp Reynolds. Here and elsewhere, there are short sidetrips for exploration. At **1.7** miles, the road swings around to expose great views of San Francisco and Alcatraz. Continue on Perimeter Rd.

2.9 Junction with Fire Road. Stay on Perimeter Road. It rises over a small ridge to reveal east bay views before dropping quickly down to East Garrison (**3.5** mi.). The road enters into the Garrison area and you must take a left turn and go by the old hospital to stay on Perimeter Rd. The old decrepit buildings are great to explore, and you can imagine the better days that they have seen.

3.9 Junction ❷ and Fire Station. Go up to the left between two buildings to climb to an upper loop FR, called "Fire Road."

4.3 Y-junction. Fire Road loop begins here. Go right. You'll pass the islands fresh water reservoirs before heading out into a delightful wooded hillside with ferns and vine-covered slopes. It is on this upper loop where you'll appreciate the biking the most, as it takes you beyond the reach of the typical tourist. You catch glimpses of Ayala Cove on this north side of the island, looking like a scene from a Mediterranean postcard. Near the 6th mile you come to the breathtaking San Francisco side; the views are fantastic!

7.2 Junction. Go left onto semipaved surface and in 100 yds., veer right onto the Fire Road again. At **7.7** miles, you hit the connecting road heading downhill. Go right.

8.0 Junction ❷ and Perimeter Rd. Turn left to complete the lower loop. At **9.2** miles, you return to the junction above Ayala Cove. Take the bike trail to the right back to the cove and dock at **9.7** miles.

Getting There

From Hwy 101:

Near Mill Valley, E on Tiburon Blvd for 3.8 miles. R on Main St to the ferry dock. Park 3 blocks earlier off of Tiburon Blvd (Fee) or 2.3 miles earlier at Blackie's Pasture. For Tiburon Ferry, call 415-435-2131.

Southern Marin

Angel Island State Park

Ayala Cove Dock

Elevation Profile

2000'

1500'

1000'

500'

4 8 12 16

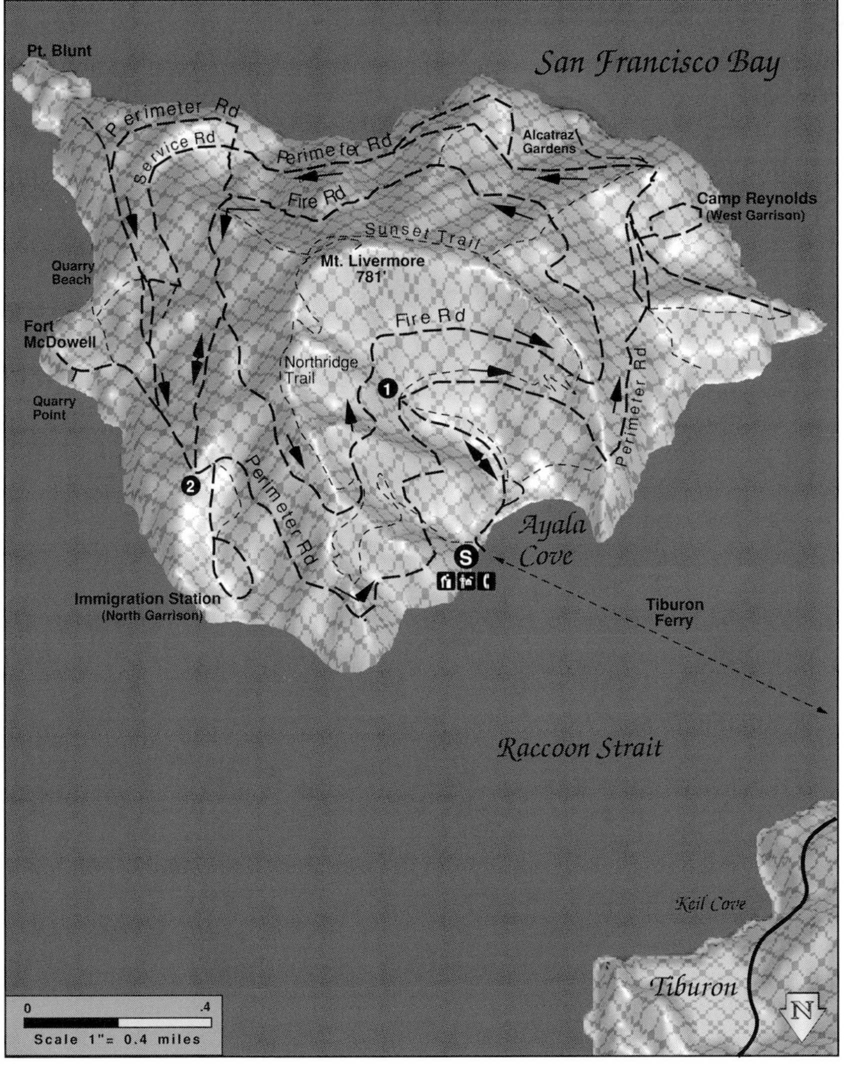

8 Warner Canyon to Corte Madera Ridge

Distance: 9.0 miles ***Riding Time:*** 1.5 hours
Elevation Change: 1400' ***Difficulty:*** Moderate to strenuous
Technical Rating: 6 Rocky climbs, some steep downhill.

A ridge ride above Mill Valley and Corte Madera. Steep ups and downs in the shadow of Mt. Tam challenge your aerobic capacity. Be sure to take in the views of SF Bay. Bring sunscreen.

0.0 From the Mill Valley Depot Cafe, take Throckmorton going east. At the second intersection turn right on Blithedale Ave and then make a quick left onto Sunnyside.

0.4 Junction ❶ with Carmelita Ave. Go left and then at **0.6** miles, right onto Buena Vista. At **1.4** miles, Buena Vista turns into Glen Dr. near the Mill Valley golf course. Ride up Glen to the end.

1.8 MCOSD protection gate. Climb the FR into Warner Canyon.

2.3 Y-junction ❷. Go left to ride along the fairly flat FR through a beautiful woodland area. This is the easy part of the ride.

3.6 Gate and junction with paved road. Go left down paved road to Elinor Ave. At Elinor (**3.8** mi.) go right up a driveway that says 1 Via Van Dyke. At **3.9** miles, go right at the Y towards a water tank. There is a small trail just past the tank. Take this trail up to Blithedale Ridge.

4.0 Junction ❸ on Blithedale Ridge. Go right to ride the challenging up and down ridge. As you gradually climb towards Mt. Tam and Corte Madera Ridge, occasionally stop and take in the view.

5.0 Junction ❹ with Corte Madera Ridge (900'). Go right to do some more up and down riding. Just ahead, look for views out to the bay.

5.7 Street. Go through the gate and zip down the paved road.

6.1 Protection gate on right. Leave the street, go through gate and descend down a fairly steep FR.

6.7 Four-way junction ❺. Go right along another fairly flat FR.

7.2 Junction with FR. Go right and climb over a small knoll before descending super steeply.

7.7 Gate and paved road. Go right on paved road which is Del Casa. At T-junction (**8.0** mi.), go left. Take Manor right (**8.3** mi.) to Buena Vista, back past the golf course.

8.5 Carmelita Ave. Go left, then a quick right onto Sunnyside back to Blithedale and on into town.

9.0 Back at the Depot Cafe and parking area.

Getting There

From Hwy 101:

Near Mill Valley, W on East Blithedale for 1.9 miles. L on Throckmorton. Park near the Depot Cafe at Miller and Throckmorton.

Southern Marin

Marin County Open Space
Downtown Mill Valley

Elevation Profile

2000'
1500'
1000'
500'
4
8
12
16

9 Old RR Grade to Blithedale Ridge

Distance: 10.7 miles *Riding Time:* 1.5 hours
Elevation Change: 1700' *Difficulty:* Moderate
Technical Rating: 6 Easy climbs, steep downhill sections.

A gentle slope up Old Railroad Grade keeps you fresh for the rollercoaster ride down loose and rocky Blithedale Ridge. Good views of San Francisco Bay with lots of sun on the ridge. A good group ride.

0.0 Start at the Mill Valley Depot Cafe. Get on Throckmorton going east. At the second intersection turn left on West Blithedale Ave and ride up on the paved road.

1.2 Junction of Old Railroad Grade. Go right past a gate over a short wooden bridge that marks the beginning of a steady FR ascent. At **1.8** miles, stay to left at junction of Horseshoe and Old Railroad. At **3.0** miles, Old Railroad Grade turns into paved Summit Rd. for half a mile.

4.1 Junction with Gravity Car Grade. Stay right on Railroad. From 1896 to 1929, the Mt. Tamalpais and Muir Woods Railway ran from Mill Valley to the top of Mt. Tam on what was known as the "Crookest Railroad in the World." Gravity cars were used to coast down to Muir Woods from this stop.

Steam Engine with Gravity Cars

4.5 Junction ❶ of Hoo-Koo-E-Koo FR and Railroad (1200'). Go right for a long, smooth, winding downhill that ends with a short ascent.

6.4 Junction ❷ with unsigned Blithedale Ridge FR. Go right and ride onto the ridge. The road first steeply descends and then rolls.

7.8 Junction ❸. Take Corte Madera Ridge to the left. About 100' down the fire road, you get a long, sweeping view down Warner Canyon and out to the bay.

7.9 Junction. Take the Glen FR downhill. At a junction at **8.4** miles, bear left downhill, through the gate and onto a paved street. Follow Glen Drive to Buena Vista Ave, then head left down the canyon and past the golf course.

10.1 Junction ❹ with Carmelita Ave. Turn left and then a quick right onto Sunnyside Ave, which takes you back to East Blithedale. Go right on East Blithedale to Throckmorton, then left to the Depot (**10.7** mi.).

Getting There

From Hwy 101:

Near Mill Valley, W on East Blithedale for 1.9 miles. L on Throckmorton. Park near the Depot Cafe at Miller and Throckmorton.

Southern Marin

Marin County Open Space
Downtown Mill Valley

Elevation Profile

2000'
1500'
1000'
500'
1
2
3
4
8
12
16

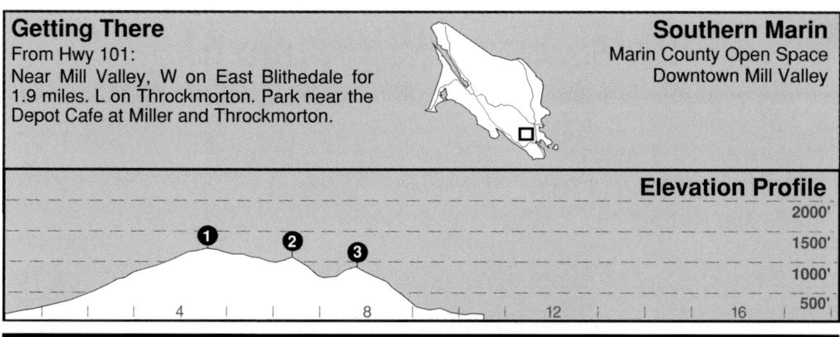

Panoramic
Tenderfoot
Old Railroad Grade
1
Eldridge
Grade
Indian FR
Hoo Koo
Koo
FR
2
Mill Valley
Old Railroad
Grade
Cascade Dr
Throckmorton
Summit Ave
Crown Rd
West Blithedale
3
Miller
S
Blithedale Ridge FR
Glen FR
Warner Canyon FR
Corte Madera Ridge FR
Sunny side
Carmelita
4
Buena Vista
Glen Dr
Mill Valley
Summit
Edison
Madrone Ave
Larkspur
Magnolia
Redwood
Camino
Sarah Dr
Alto FR
Corte Madera
0
.6
Scale 1" = 0.6 miles
N

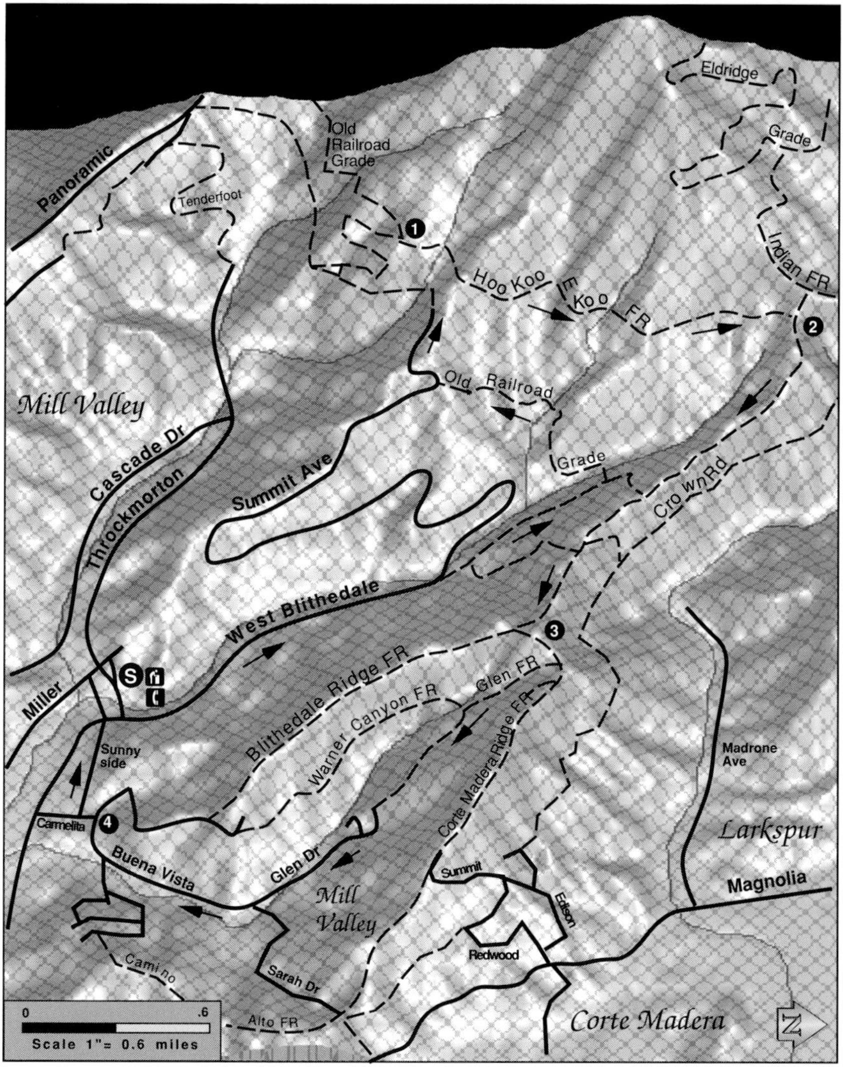

10 Old RR Grade to West Point Inn

Distance: 13.2 miles *Riding Time:* 1.5-2 hours
Elevation Change: 1700' *Difficulty:* Moderate
Technical Rating: 5 Fairly good fire road with moderate grade. A medium-sized out and back ride for advanced beginners and intermediates, with good views along the way. This ride opens the door to many options on the south side of Mt. Tam.

0.0 From downtown Mill Valley, ride north on Throckmorton to the intersection of W. Blithedale Rd. (**0.1** mi.). Go left out W. Blithedale. The road is narrow and can be busy. Continue past Blithedale Park.

1.2 Protection gate. Go right to head up on Old Railroad Grade. This FR is uniquely gradual, with a grade never exceeding 7%, because it once had trains running up to the peak of Mt. Tam. At **1.9** miles, veer left at the fork. The trail enters a paved residential area for about one-half mile at **3.1** miles. Stay on the uphill road.

4.2 Island junction ❶ with Gravity Car Grade. Continue right on Old Railroad Grade towards West Point Inn. The FR does a series of gradual switchbacks here known as the "double bowknot."

6.6 Junction ❷ and West Point Inn (1790'). This historic railroad tavern, built in 1904, was a restaurant, inn, and transfer point for the stage to Bolinas. It has a few surviving buildings that have been rescued by a group of volunteers who restore and preserve it. West Point Inn is also available for overnight stays, group parties and occasional Sunday pancake breakfasts in the summer. Take some time to rest and enjoy the scenery and the history of the Inn before returning the way you came to Mill Valley at **13.2** miles.

West Point Inn

Options: There are several options for additional riding from here. You can continue on the Old Railroad Grade up to the East Peak, then ride along Ridgecrest Blvd. to Rock Spring, then down to Pantoll. Or you can take the Old Stage Rd. to Pantoll (not shown on the map). At Pantoll, you can take Panoramic Hwy to the Mtn. Home Inn. However, weekend or commute-time traffic can be heavy and nasty.

Getting There

From Hwy 101:

Near Mill Valley, W on East Blithedale for 1.9 miles, L on Throckmorton. Park near the Depot Cafe at Miller and Throckmorton.

Southern Marin

Marin County Open Space
Downtown Mill Valley

Elevation Profile
2000'
1500'
1000'
500'
4
8
12
16

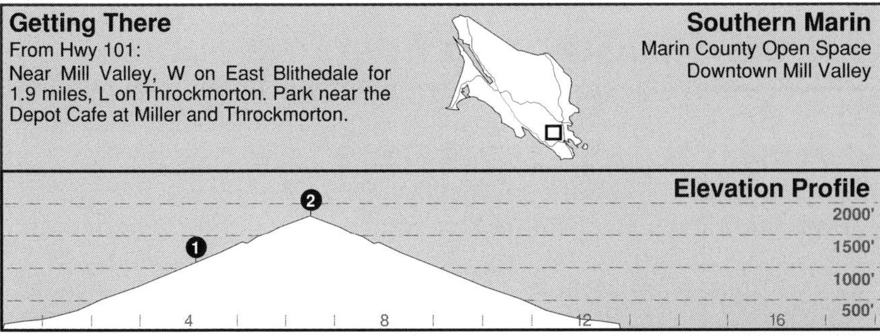

West Point Inn
1785'
Panoramic Hwy
E Ridgecrest
Eldridge Grade
East Peak
2571'
Old Railroad Grade
Gravity Car
Mtn Home Inn
920'
Tenderfoot Trail
Hoo Koo E Koo
Indian Fire Trail
Lovell
Cascade Drive
Old Railroad Grade
Summit Ave
Southern Marin Line FR
Cascade Drive
Throckmorton
West Blithedale
Blithedale Ridge FR
Miller
Depot
0
.7
Scale 1" = 0.7 miles
N

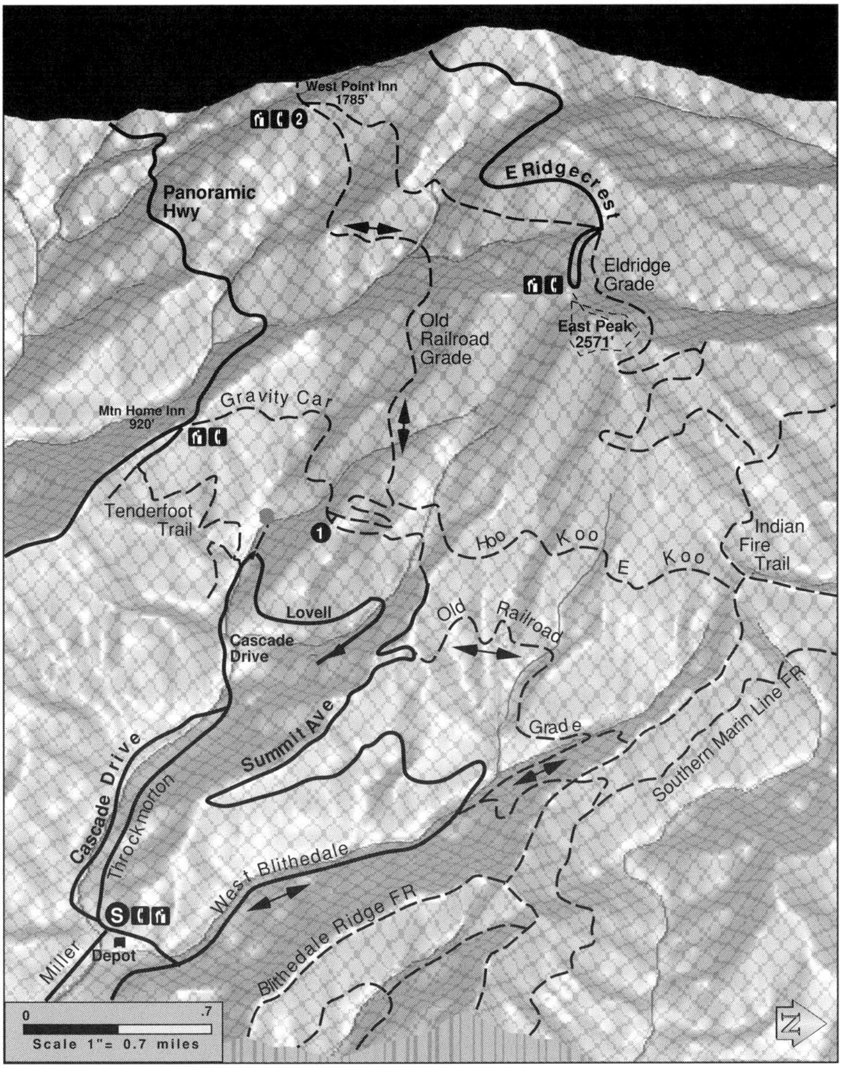

11 Old RR Grade to East Peak Loop

Distance: 18.0 miles ***Riding Time:*** 2.5-3 hours
Elevation Change: 2700' ***Difficulty:*** Strenuous
Technical Rating: 10 Rocky fire road descent, technical single track. A gradual, but long ascent brings you to Marin's highest point, Mt. Tam's East Peak. The trip down includes some radical technical fire road sections and ends with a superb single track. Five Stars.

0.0 Take Throckmorton going east. At the 2nd intersection turn left on West Blithedale Ave and continue up on the paved road.

1.1 Junction ❶ with Old Railroad Grade. Go past the gate and over the wooden bridge and begin a gentle FR ascent of Mt. Tam.

4.1 Junction ❷ with Gravity Car Grade. Stay right on Railroad.

4.4 Junction ❸ with Hoo-Koo-E-Koo FR (loop returns here). Stay left.

6.4 West Point Inn. Wind right around the structures and up.

7.9 Junction ❹ with Ridgecrest Blvd and Eldridge Grade. Go right up the one-way paved road to East Peak. A panoramic view is your reward. The soda vending machine (take bills and coins) and a food stand (open on weekends in the spring and summer) don't hurt either. When done, head back down to Eldridge Grade.

8.6 Junction ❹ again with Eldridge Grade. Go down. This is the beginning of a rocky technical descent. Flat tire central! Be light on the bike and watch for others. About 0.5 mile, a path to the left leads to a large rock that has great views and basking conditions.

11.1 Junction ❺ with Indian FT. Make a hairpin right down Indian FT. After a few turns the road straightens out, and gets steep and nasty. Just as the nasty stuff ends, watch for a road on the right.

11.7 Junction with Blithedale Ridge. Go right and in about 100' make another right onto Hoo-Koo-E-Koo FR to climb back to Old Railroad.

13.7 Junction ❸ with Old Railroad Grade. Go left downhill.

14.0 Junction ❷. Take Gravity Car right towards Mtn. Home Inn.

15.0 Junction ❻ with Panoramic Hwy. Go left 100', then left down Edgewood Ave. At **15.5** miles, take the Tenderfoot trail on the left. (If Edgewood becomes a dirt trail, you went 100 yds. too far.) This descent is the one of the most technical, legal single tracks in Marin. Slippery roots, drop-offs and tight sections make it a challenge.

16.8 Bottom of Tenderfoot at Cascade Dr. Go right and follow Cascade back into downtown Mill Valley (**18.0** miles).

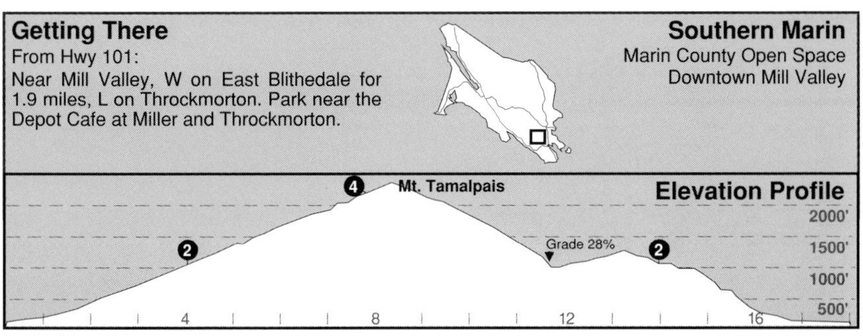

Getting There

From Hwy 101:

Near Mill Valley, W on East Blithedale for 1.9 miles, L on Throckmorton. Park near the Depot Cafe at Miller and Throckmorton.

Southern Marin

Marin County Open Space
Downtown Mill Valley

Elevation Profile
Mt. Tamalpais
Grade 28%
2000'
1500'
1000'
500'
4
8
12
16

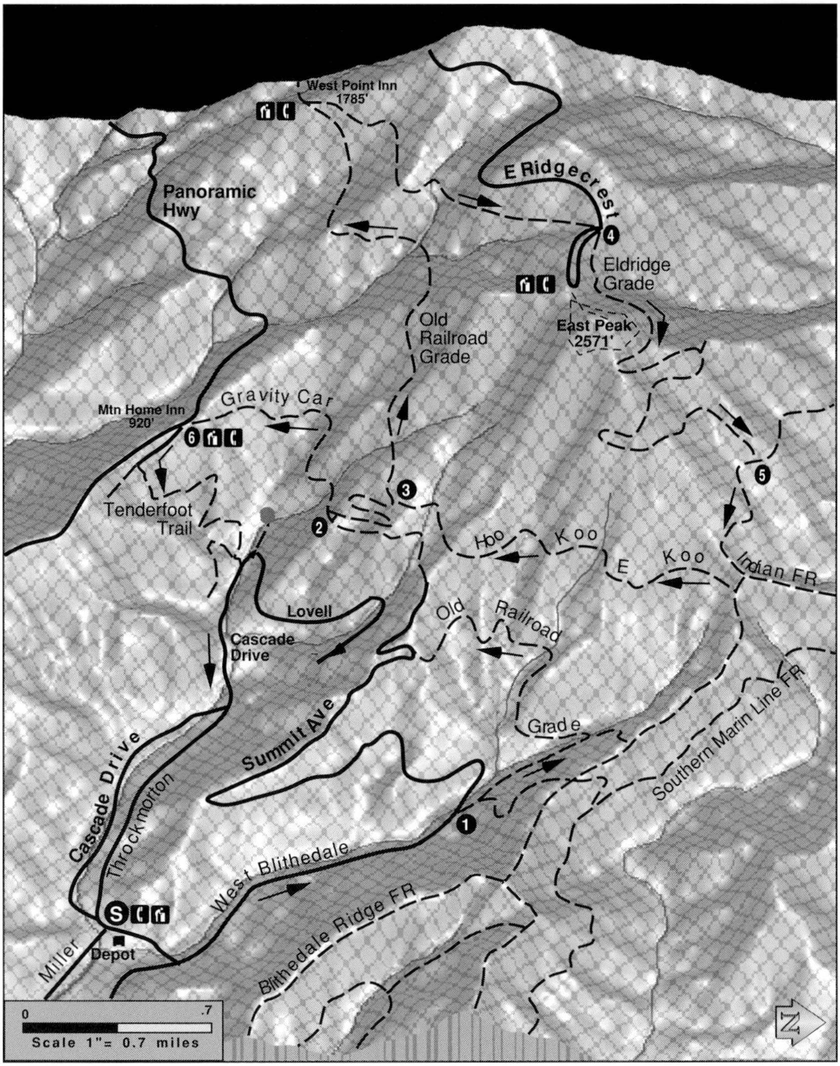

West Point Inn
1785'
Panoramic Hwy
E Ridgecrest
Eldridge Grade
East Peak
2571'
Old Railroad Grade
Gravity Car
Mtn Home Inn
920'
6
Tenderfoot Trail
Hoo Koo E Koo
Indian FR
Lovell
Cascade Drive
Old Railroad Grade
Summit Ave
Southern Marin Line FR
Cascade Drive
Throckmorton
West Blithedale
Blithedale Ridge FR
S
Miller
Depot
0
.7
Scale 1" = 0.7 miles
N

12 Muir Woods to Pantoll Loop

Distance: 9.5 miles ***Riding Time:*** 1-1.5 hours
Elevation Change: 1500' ***Difficulty:*** Moderate to strenuous
Technical Rating: 7 Some steep climbing and a gnarly descent.
Privacy, splendid ocean views, and little-used trails are the payoff for the remote start. This ride makes a fairly steep climb along the famed Dipsea trail, then a fast drop down Coastal trail. Watch your speed.

0.0 Ride up the Deer Park FR on the west side of Muir Woods Rd. The climb is fairly steep and takes you through fir forests up a ridge towards Mt. Tamalpais. The Dipsea trail, of the famed footrace, winds in and out of the FR. At **1.9** miles, the FR goes through an ancient redwood burn zone. The deep green chain ferns you see here are stunning against the blackened bark of the burnt redwoods. Rest at the small landing here before resuming the steep climb.

2.5 Junction ❶ of Coastal Trail (1300'). The view from here is incredible on clear days. You can see Diaz Ridge to the south, Ocean Beach of San Francisco, big ships heading towards the gate, and the Farallon Islands to the northwest. Continue up to the right towards Pantoll. At **2.6** miles, another Y-junction marks a turn off to Lone Tree Trail, a very steep FR to Hwy 1. Stay right. At **2.9** miles, the FR comes into the corporation yard for Mt. Tam State Park. Ride through the yard to the parking area for Pantoll.

3.2 Junction ❷ with Pantoll Ranger Station (1500'). We turn around here, so touch the gate and head on back to the Coastal trail.

3.8 Junction ❶ again. Go right to begin the gnarly drop to Hwy 1. At present, the FR is unmaintained. After the El Nino winter of 1998, it had huge ruts and crevasses just waiting to swallow up your front wheel. At **5.2** miles, a super steep section falls away onto a small lookout point, where you can see a ribbon of Hwy 1 clinging to the cliffs above the ocean. This is a phenomenal sunset ride! At **5.9** mi. go around gate and ride the last little section of rough two track.

6.2 Junction ❸ with Hwy 1. Go left on Hwy 1 along the bluffs before dropping down towards Muir Beach (**6.6** mi.).

7.6 Junction of Muir Woods Rd. Go left for the gentle climb back to the start. It's a paved road that winds through beautiful Franks Valley.

Option: It's worth a short detour right to visit Muir Beach.

9.5 Back at the parking area.

Getting There

From Hwy 101:

Near Sausalito, W on Hwy 1 for 3.3 miles, R on Panoramic Hwy for 0.9 miles. L on Muir Woods Rd. Go past Muir Woods 0.7 miles and park near the FR on the right.

Southern Marin

Mt. Tamalpais State Park
Muir Woods Area

Elevation Profile

2000'	
1500'	
1000'	
500'	

Distance: 4, 8, 12, 16

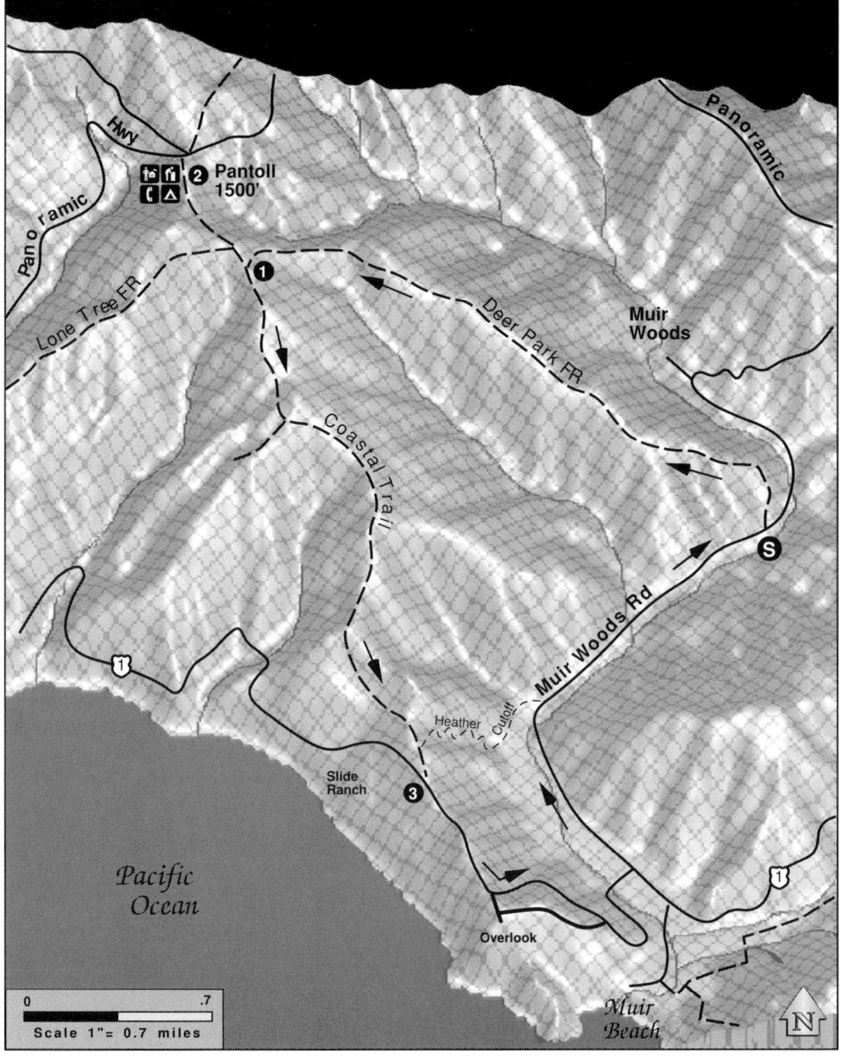

13 Rock Spring to Laurel Dell Loop

Distance: 5.4 miles ***Riding Time:*** About 1 hour
Elevation Change: 800' ***Difficulty:*** Easy to moderate
Technical Rating: 4 Good fire roads; some paved roads
A leisurely ride through mountain meadows, streams and forests. Good picnic areas along the way. On clear days, take in the views of the ocean at Stinson Beach and Bolinas. Watch for hang gliders.

0.0 Start at Rock Spring parking area and head left to ride up Ridgecrest Blvd towards the east.

0.3 Entrance to Mountain Theater. Head right to explore the theater. It is a fantastic gothic-feeling stone amphitheater that was built in 1934 using over 40,000 stones. Each stone is buried so that only a fraction is visible. Plays are held 6-8 Sunday afternoons starting in late May. You can catch rehearsals (free) on the Saturdays before each play. Also, check out a small knoll with extra large trees on it. The knoll is located on a spur road 100 yds. to the right of the road to the theater. After exploring, head back out to Ridgecrest Blvd.

Mountain Theater

0.7 Junction ❶. Just past the Mountain Theater, take the first FR left, the Rock Spring-Lagunitas FR. The road makes a short steep climb up to a saddle and then drops down to Potrero Meadows.

1.6 Junction ❷ at the southwest end of Potrero Meadows. Go left down Laurel Dell FR. At **1.7** miles, Potrero Camp is on the right. It's another secluded spot to enjoy a private meadow with a picnic bench and a small stream. The FR continues mostly downhill.

3.3 Laurel Dell. After a steady descent, the forest opens up to a long narrow meadow with a stream (Cataract Creek) coming in from the left. Cross the creek, then the FR climbs up to Bolinas Ridge. **Note**: There are some nice waterfalls downstream about 0.5 miles.

3.9 Junction ❸ at West Ridgecrest Blvd. Go left along the paved road to truck it back to the start. The road has some climbing. Along the way, watch for hang gliders that take off from the ridge.

5.4 Back at the Rock Spring parking area. It's worth a short hike to the south to the serpentine rocky hilltop for more great coastal views.

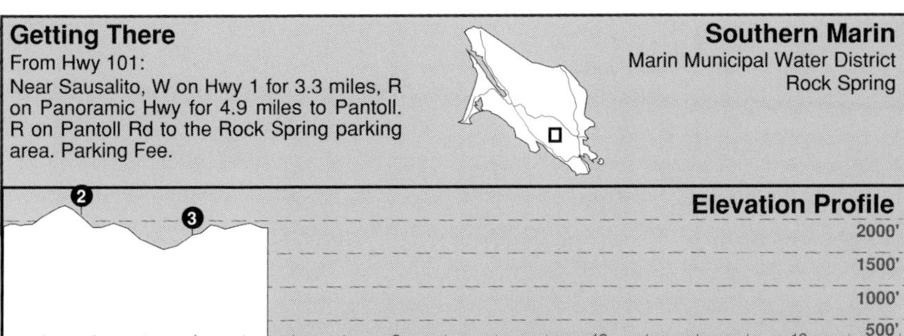

Getting There

From Hwy 101:
Near Sausalito, W on Hwy 1 for 3.3 miles, R on Panoramic Hwy for 4.9 miles to Pantoll. R on Pantoll Rd to the Rock Spring parking area. Parking Fee.

Southern Marin

Marin Municipal Water District
Rock Spring

Elevation Profile
2000'
1500'
1000'
500'
4
8
12
16
2
3

Willow Camp Fr
Ridgecrest Blvd
Laurel Dell
Cataract Trail
Laurel Dell FR
O'Rourkes Bench
Barths Retreat
Potrero Camp
Benstein Trail
Pantoll Rd
Rock Spring
Potrero Meadows
Rock Spring
Lagunitas
Mtn Theater
Ridgecrest Blvd
FR
Rifle Camp
S
1
2
3
0
.4
Scale 1"= 0.4 miles
N

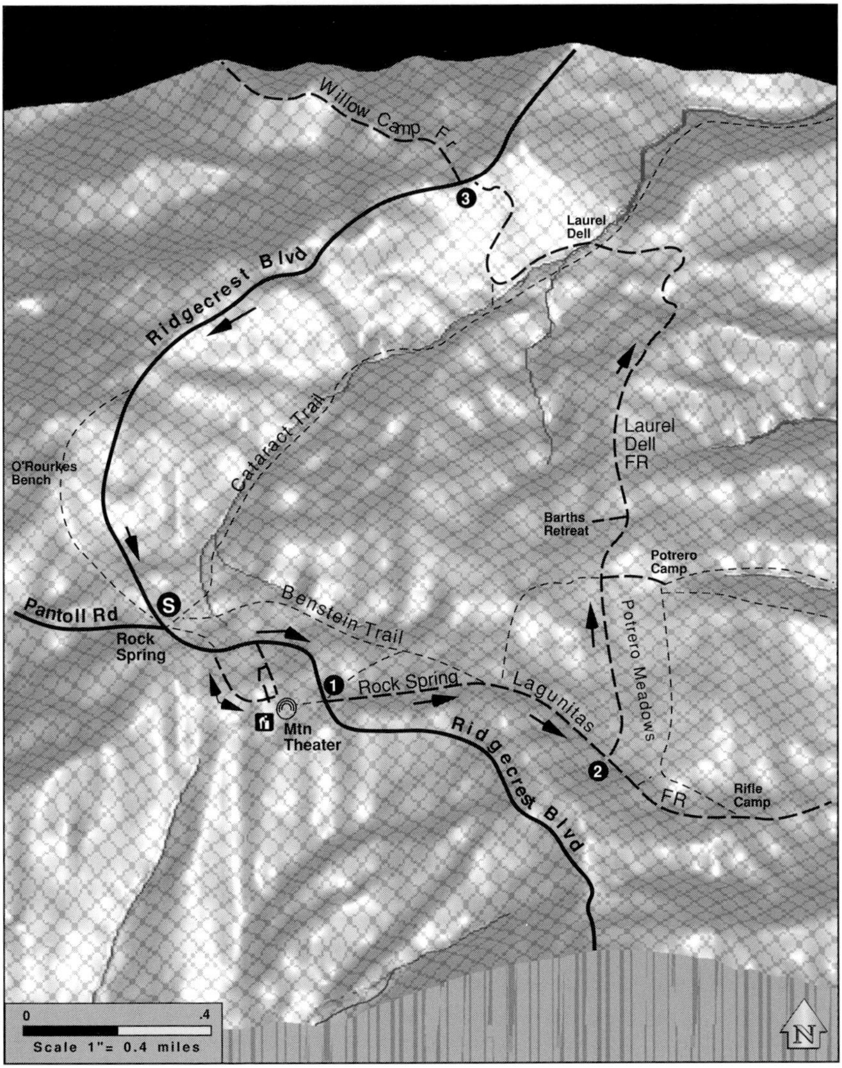

14 Bald Hill Loop

Distance: 5.8 miles ***Riding Time:*** 1 hour
Elevation Change: 1200' ***Difficulty:*** Moderate
Technical Rating: 6 A very steep, sometimes nasty descent.
A peak-bag ride to the summit of Bald Hill in the heart of the Ross Valley. Lake views and choice vistas from this treeless hill make this short ride a worthy jaunt. Bring sunscreen. Some paved road.

0.0 Start at Ross Common. Ride towards Lagunitas Rd. and turn left. Stay on Lagunitas Rd. through two stop signs.

0.7 Junction ❶ and stop sign at Glenwood Dr. Go right and then quick left on Upper Rd. Upper Road takes you through shady woods and up past some elegant Ross estates.

1.1 Y-junction with Upper Rd. West. Go left at this fork. At **1.5** mi. the paved road ends and you head out into MMWD open space through a gate onto FR. The climb is moderately steep, but shady with pockets of deep shade in the redwoods. At **1.9** mi., the FR goes out onto open hillsides and offers views of the northeast Ross Valley.

2.4 Saddle and T-junction ❷. An unexpected vista of Mt. Tamalpais greets you at the saddle. Go left to make the last of the ascent to the top of Bald Hill. At **2.5** miles, go left again to the open summit.

Bald Hill from Eldridge Grade

2.5 Summit of Bald Hill (1141') and viewpoint. The 360° views of the Ross Valley and the hills beyond are exceptional. To continue,backtrack 100 yds., then bear left to head down into the Phoenix Lake drainage basin. The trail is extremely steep, loose, and off-camber. Speed can be treacherous here, so be careful. The almost 2 miles of downhill you get here is challenging and well worth the climb. Baldy's sweeping grassy hillsides are always beautiful, but they are especially colorful in the spring when the hills are green.

4.3 Junction ❸ with Phoenix Lake. Go left to the dam, then downhill. **Option**: You can add a pleasant mile by staying on the FR to the end.

4.7 Base of dam. Ride out of the parking lot towards the main road. Continue on Lagunitas Rd. back to the car at **5.8** miles.

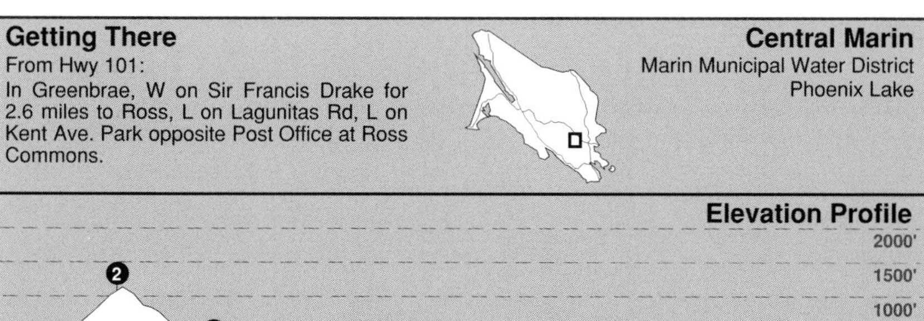
Getting There
From Hwy 101:
In Greenbrae, W on Sir Francis Drake for 2.6 miles to Ross, L on Lagunitas Rd, L on Kent Ave. Park opposite Post Office at Ross Commons.
Central Marin
Marin Municipal Water District
Phoenix Lake
Elevation Profile
2000'
1500'
1000'
500'
4
8
12
16
Sir Francis Drake Blvd
Bolinas
Fairfax
Butterfield Rd
San Francisco Blvd
Cascade Dr
Center Blvd
Deer Park Rd
Red Hill Ave
San Anselmo
SF Drake Blvd
Deer Park FR
Bald Hill 1141'
Upper West
Bolinas Rd
Five Corners
Six Points
Worn
Glenwood Dr
Yolanda Trail
Springs Rd
Upper Rd
Lagunitas Rd
Kent Av
Ross
Shaver Grade
Fish Grade
Natalie Greene Park
Phoenix Lake
Lake Lagunitas
Scale 1"= 0.6 miles

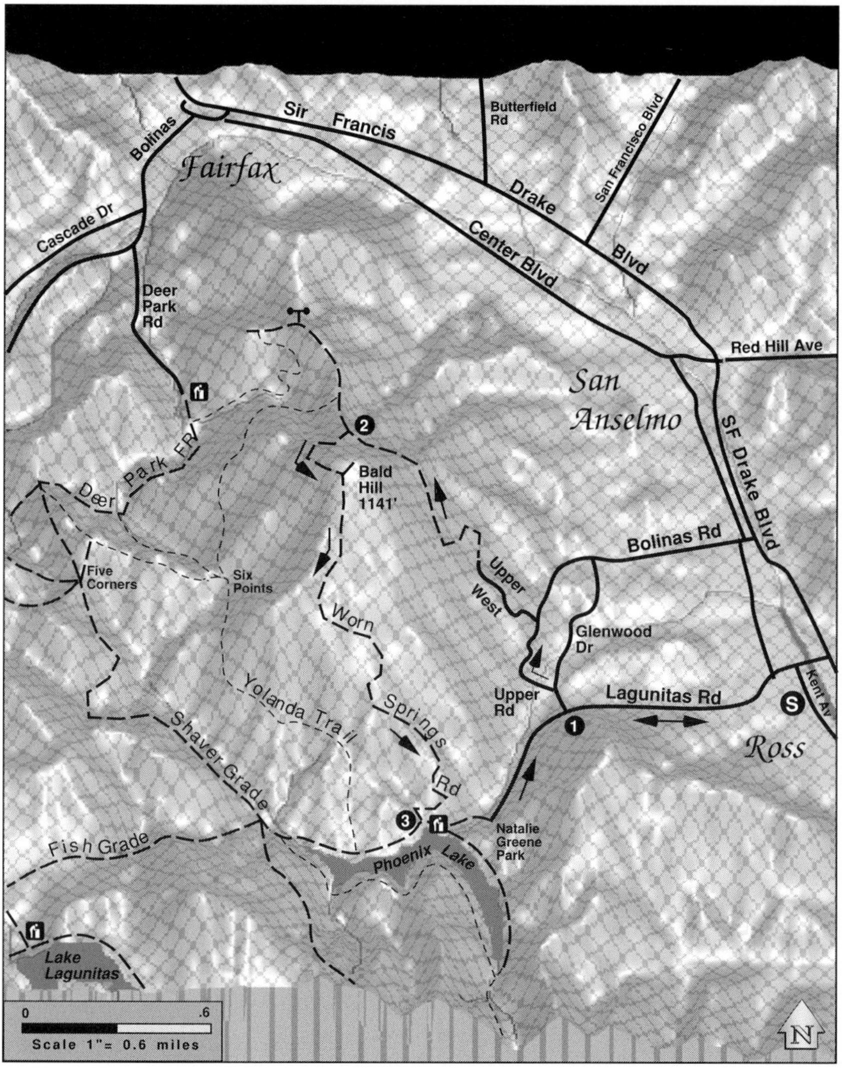

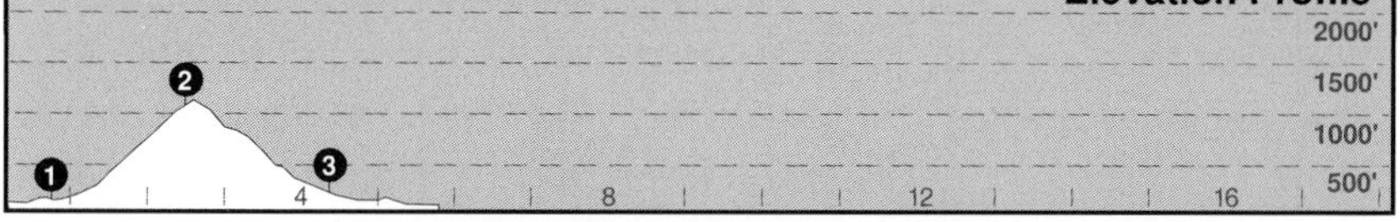

15 Shaver Grade - Bullfrog Rd. Loop

Distance: 10.2 miles ***Riding Time:*** 1-1.5 hours
Elevation Change: 1050' ***Difficulty:*** Easy to moderate
Technical Rating: 3 Fairly good fire roads.
This ride takes you past three lakes and Bon Tempe meadow in the Marin Municipal Water District. It has moderate climbing and is a good beginner/intermediate ride. Some mud in winter.

0.0 From Ross Common, ride to Lagunitas Rd. and go left to take the paved road to Natalie Coffin Greene Park.

1.1 Parking lot. Go up the FR to the dam. Continue straight at the dam to follow the FR counter-clockwise around lake.

2.0 Four-way junction ❶. Take the right FR, Shaver Grade, which is a well traveled, but tranquil FR that starts to climb in about one-half mile. It is mostly shaded by a canopy of redwoods, oaks and bays. At **2.7** miles, Pipeline FR leaves to the left, keep climbing.

3.1 Junction ❷ at Five Corners. Ride up to the left, staying on Shaver. The FR climbs in two short steep sections to a paved road.

3.7 Top of Shaver and junction ❸. Take the paved, unsigned Sky Oaks Rd. to the right. After about a 100', go left onto a gravel road that heads down to Bon Tempe and Alpine lakes.

4.2 Gate. Alpine Lake laps along the bank of this FR making a sheltered nursery for frogs, and a water source for jackrabbits that you might see in the early morning. Bullfrog road takes you up over a knoll to an old quarry where rock was obtained to build Bon Tempe dam. Come down into a grassy meadow, and stay on the right side of the meadow on the main FR. This road can get soggy in the winter.

5.1 Junction ❹ with Sky Oaks Rd. Go left to follow the paved road past the Sky Oaks ranger station, and down towards the main road.

5.4 Junction ❺ with Fairfax-Bolinas Rd. Go right and right again at a FR behind another MMWD gate. This is Concrete Pipe FR, which follows the contours of the hillside.

6.9 Junction ❷ at Five Corners. Retrace your ride to return back from here. Shaver is the 2nd left and in 0.2 mile, stay left. The moderate grade allows you to really pick up speed here, but stay under 15 mph, and slow down at the corners, some of which are sharp.

8.0 Four-way junction ❶. Take the left to return along Phoenix Lake and back to the parking area (**10.2** miles).

Getting There

From Hwy 101:

In Greenbrae, W on Sir Francis Drake for 2.6 miles to Ross, L on Lagunitas Rd, L on Kent Ave. Park opposite Post Office at Ross Common.

Central Marin

Marin Municipal Water District

Phoenix Lake

Elevation Profile

2000'
1500'
1000'
500'
4 8 12 16

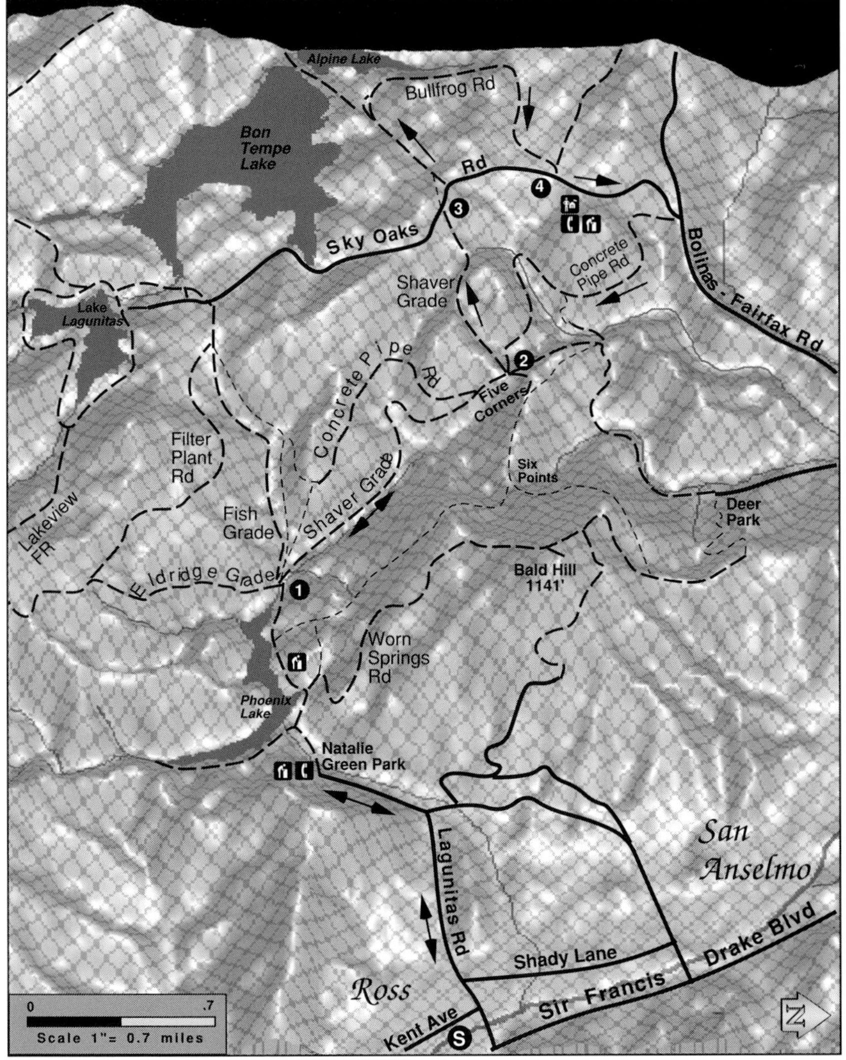

16 Eldridge Grade – Lake Lagunitas

Distance: 11.2 miles ***Riding Time:*** 1.5-2 hours
Elevation Change: 1000' ***Difficulty:*** Moderate
Technical Rating: 5 Short section of steep, rocky terrain.

A fire road ride through riparian woodlands, redwood forests and grasslands make this a very popular area with bikers, hikers, and horseback riders. Abundant bird life and turtles at the lake.

0.0 From Ross Common, ride to Lagunitas Road and go left. Stay on Lagunitas through three stop signs.

1.1 Parking lot of Natalie Coffin Greene Park (130'). Go right across a two-track bridge and up the fire road.

1.4 Junction ❶ at the top of the dam. Continue straight, past the ranger house and counter-clockwise around Phoenix Lake. At **1.5** miles, there's a water spigot on the right. At **1.6** miles, you'll pass the junction of Worn Springs Road.

2.0 Four-way junction ❷. Go left up Eldridge Grade. Fish Gulch is straight and very steep, Shaver Grade is right (the return route).

2.8 T-junction and water spigot. Go left and continue up Eldridge, This road was built as a toll road by John C. Eldridge in the 1880s, providing the first wagon road to the summit. It has suffered many slides and is now maintained as a trail.

3.3 Y-junction. Go either way, left is easier.

4.1 Junction ❸ with Lakeview FR (1000'). This is the highest point on the ride. Go right down Lakeview towards Lake Lagunitas. Just 0.1 mi. ahead, there is a a small plateau with oak trees on the right, offering a great rest spot with valley views, and Mt. Tam towering above.

4.7 Junction ❹ just above the lake. Take the FR left down to a vernal creek feeding Lake Lagunitas and circle the lake clockwise.

5.8 Lagunitas dam. Cross the dam and head left down the FR. Ride through the parking lot and exit on a paved road. At **6.3** miles, the road makes a 90° left turn. Stay on this main road. (The other road goes downhill and catches Fish Gulch FR, a fast, steep way back).

7.4 Junction ❺ with Shaver Grade. Go right down a gated FR.

8.1 Five Corners junction. Take the first right down, then 0.2 mile ahead at the junction with Concrete Pipe FR, bear left.

9.2 Junction ❷. Go left along the lake, then down at the dam.

11.2 Back at Ross Common.

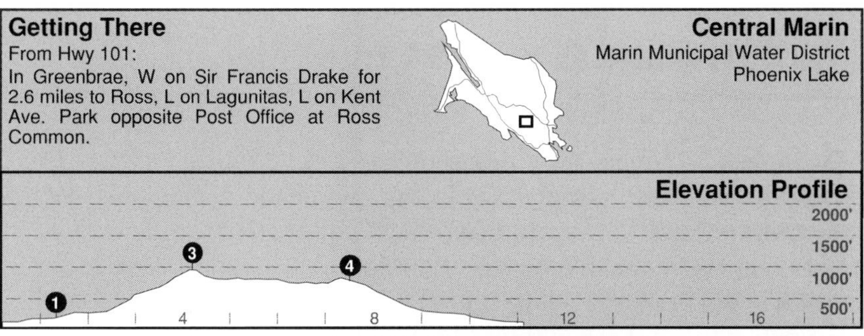

Getting There

From Hwy 101:

In Greenbrae, W on Sir Francis Drake for 2.6 miles to Ross, L on Lagunitas, L on Kent Ave. Park opposite Post Office at Ross Common.

Central Marin

Marin Municipal Water District
Phoenix Lake

Elevation Profile

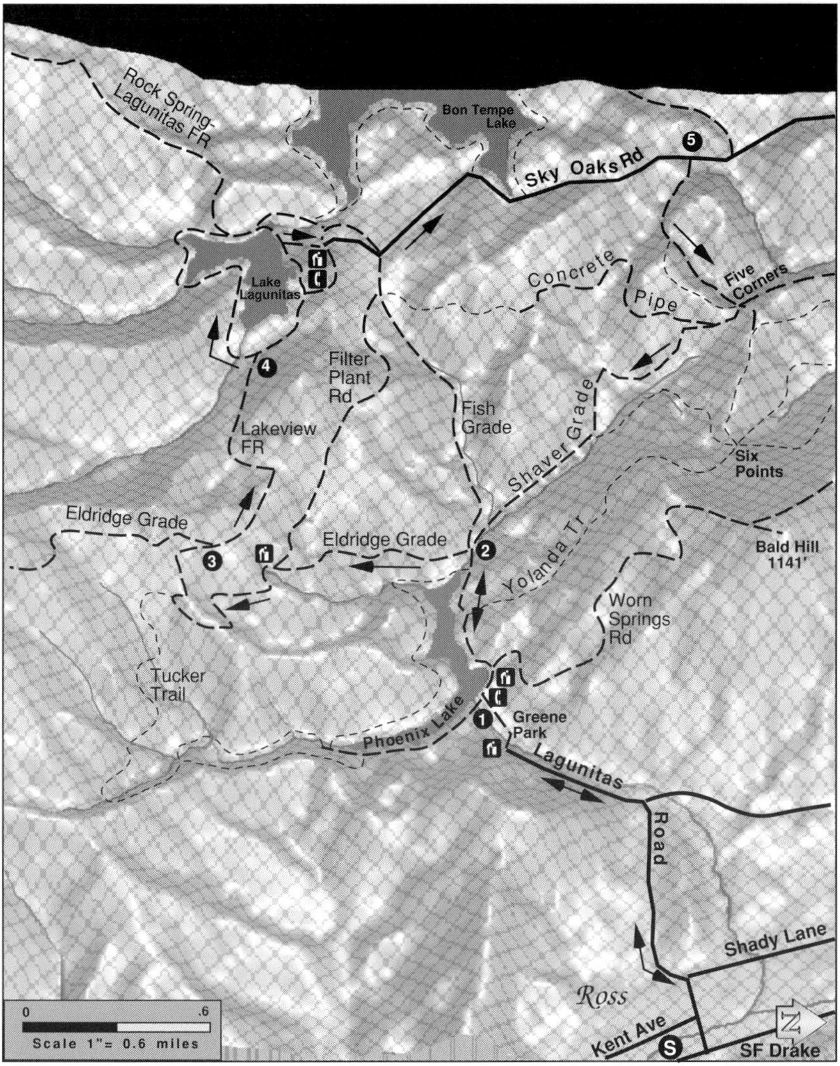

17 Eldridge Grade to East Peak Loop

Distance: 17.7 miles ***Riding Time:*** 2.5-3 hours
Elevation Change: 2800' ***Difficulty:*** Moderate to strenuous
Technical Rating: 8 Some technical climbing over rocky terrain.
Ride up rugged Eldridge Grade to the top of Mt. Tam. The long climb has wilderness appeal and panoramic views of the bay. The ride down is steep and fast. Lake and meadow rest stops. Some paved road.

0.0 From Ross Common, take Lagunitas Rd. left to Natalie Coffin Greene Park. Continue up the dirt road and head right at the dam.

2.0 Four-way junction ❶. Take the left FR to go up Eldridge Grade. This begins your long, but moderately-graded climb through redwood forests and chaparral. At **2.8** miles, turn left at the T-junction with Filter Plant FR (water available here).

4.1 Junction ❷ with Lakeview Rd. Continue up Eldridge to the left.

5.2 Junction with Indian FR. Go right. Rocky terrain ahead.

7.7 Junction ❸ with Ridgecrest Blvd. You made it! You should definitely head left up to East Peak, where there are incredible views and a snack shop (open on weekends) or a coke machine to treat yourself. The actual pinnacle is a short hike from the snack bar. Bring a bike lock if you plan to do this, no bikes are allowed on the trail. When ready, head back along Ridgecrest Blvd. past Eldridge to follow the paved road as it rolls up and down. Watch for cars here.

9.1 Junction ❹ of Rock Spring-Lagunitas FR. This is an easy junction to miss because it's off a fast downhill section. So keep your eye out for a short single track on the right that climbs to a knoll where the FR is marked by an old wooden sign. Ahead, pass by Laurel Dell FR on the left to enter Portrero Meadow (**9.9** mi.). Continue around the meadow to Rifle Camp. The FR from Rifle Camp starts steeply down the mountain. Stay in control. Be sure to stay right all the way down. The FR ends at Lake Lagunitas.

12.4 Junction ❺ with Lake Lagunitas FR. Turn left to ride to Lagunitas Dam. Cross the dam, ride down the FR to the parking lot and out along the paved road.

14.0 Junction ❻ with Shaver Grade. Turn right to go around a gate, then down Shaver Grade FR. This sends you back to Phoenix Lake.

14.6 Five Corners. Take the right FR and in 0.2 mi. veer left downhill.

15.7 Junction ❶. Go left to backtrack to the parking area at **17.7** mi.

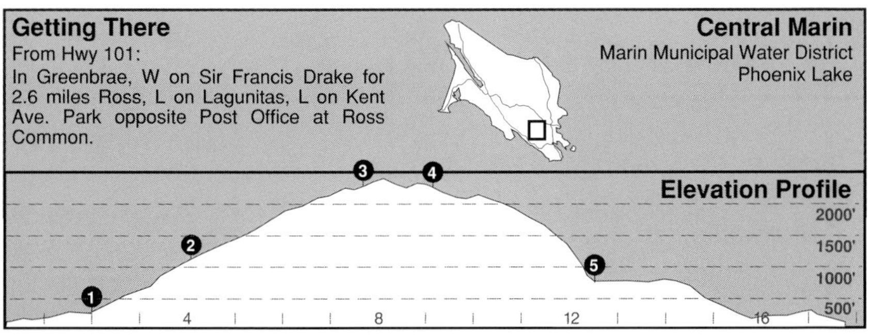

Getting There

From Hwy 101:

In Greenbrae, W on Sir Francis Drake for 2.6 miles Ross, L on Lagunitas, L on Kent Ave. Park opposite Post Office at Ross Common.

Central Marin

Marin Municipal Water District
Phoenix Lake

Elevation Profile

2000'
1500'
1000'
500'
4
8
12
16
1
2
3
4
5

Rock Spring
Mountain Theater
4
Rock Spring-Lagunitas FR
West Point Inn
Old Railroad Grade
Ridgecrest Blvd
Laurel Dell FR
Rock Spring-Lagunitas FR
Hoo Koo E Koo
East Peak 2571'
3
Rifle Camp
Grade
Northside Trail
Eldridge
Inspiration Point
Lagoon FR
Serpentine Knoll 1560'
Eldridge Grade
Indian FR
Rock Spring-Lagunitas FR
2
Lakeview
Rocky Ridge FR
Lake Lagunitas
5
Eldridge Grade
Filter Plant Rd
Crown Rd
Eldridge Grade
Sky Oaks Rd
FishGulch
Bon Tempe Lake
Phoenix Lake
1
Shaver Gr
S
Lagunitas Rd
Shaver Gr
6
Shady Lane
FiveCorners
Bullfrog Rd
Bald Hill
0
.8
Scale 1"= 0.8 miles
N

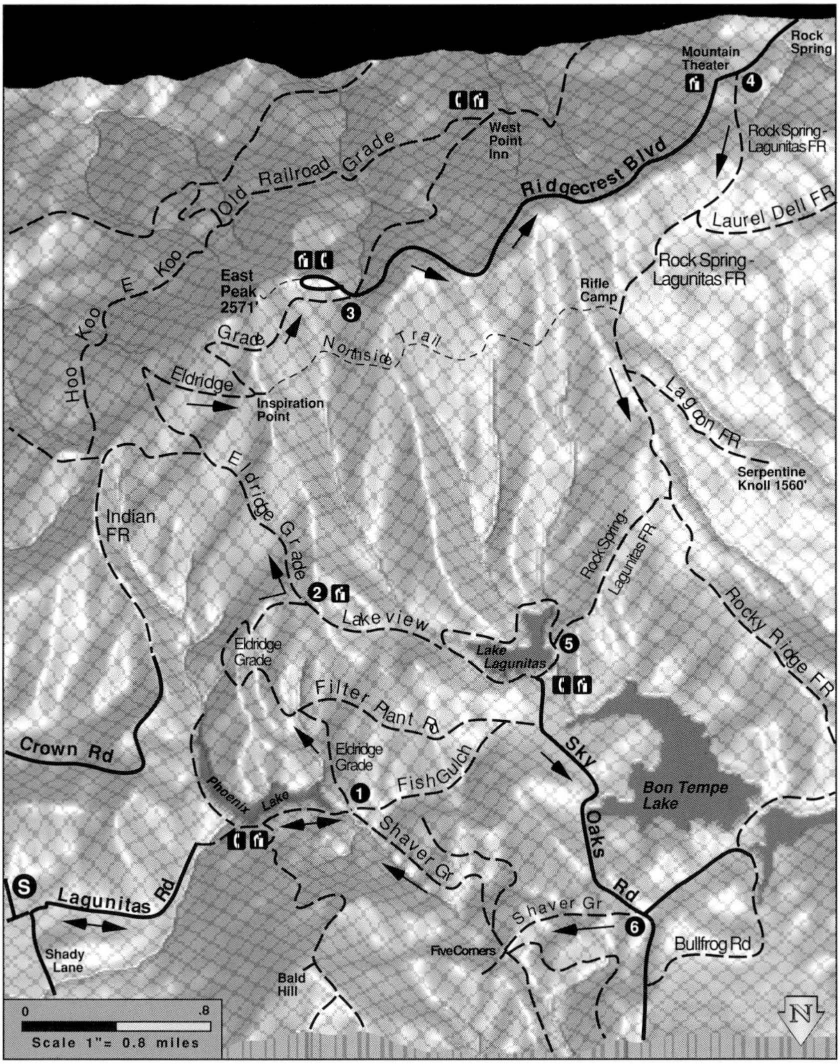

18 Camp Tamarancho - White Hill Loop

Distance: 12.5 miles ***Riding Time:*** 2-2.5 hours
Elevation Change: 1900' ***Difficulty:*** Moderate to strenuous
Technical Rating: 9 Narrow single track and steep tricky descents.

This is quintessential Marin riding! Narrow, technical, single track through tight forests and grassland. Include a short climb to bag White Hill and a quick, steep fire road descent to round out your ride.

Note: You must purchase an annual pass "Friends of Tamarancho" to ride these trails. Call 415-454-1081 for information.

0.0 From downtown Fairfax, head northwest on Broadway, then left on Azalea, right on Scenic, right on Manor, left on Rock Ridge Rd., which turns into Iron Springs Rd. at **0.7** mile.

2.4 Junction ❶ and entrance to Camp Tamarancho (680'). Head left.

3.1 Junction ❷. At the four-way junction, go right onto a maintained single track that takes you down into a creek drainage. There are several other trails here, just stay on the main one, which is challenging and fun as you wind up through the trees.

4.1 Junction ❸ with FR. Take a left turn and in 20 yds., go right onto the next single track. The Wagon Wheel trail heads onto a west-facing slope that contours the hill. Trail is narrow and has tough rocky parts.

5.5 Junction ❹. Go straight over the saddle onto a steep, short downhill FR, then take the trail on the left into shaded oak woodland and redwood forest. The trail is narrow and switchbacks in spots, a challenge to navigate without touching down.

6.6 Y-junction. Either way will work, right is easier.

6.7 Junction ❺. Go left on FR to circle around White Hill.

7.5 Junction. Head left again for a short steep climb to the top.

8.0 White Hill at 1430'. Great 360° views. Head down steep trail.

8.6 Junction ❹, your choice. Repeat single track or go straight on FR.

9.0 Junction ❸. Take FR 100 yds. east then go right to drop down a super steep FR into Cascade Canyon. **Note:** In rainy season, if creeks are flowing heavily (see below), backtrack to junction ❷ and either go left to Iron Springs Rd. or right to Toyon Dr. to complete ride.

9.8 T-junction ❻. Go right. Just ahead, a difficult rocky section.

10.2 Junction at canyon floor. Head left on the FR along Cascade Creek, which must be crossed 4 times. Continue out to Cascade Drive, then left on Bolinas Rd. to the starting area (**12.5** mi.).

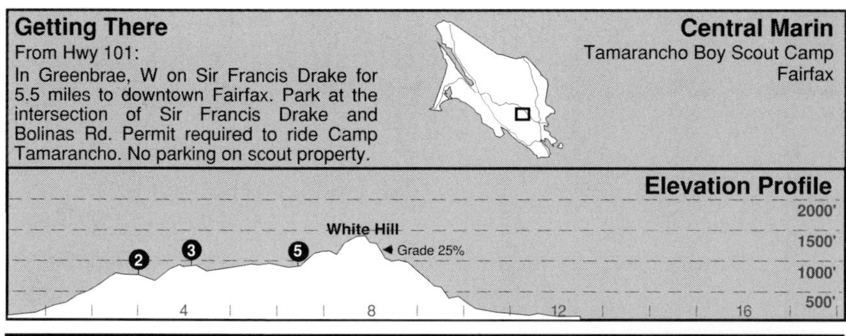

Getting There

From Hwy 101:

In Greenbrae, W on Sir Francis Drake for 5.5 miles to downtown Fairfax. Park at the intersection of Sir Francis Drake and Bolinas Rd. Permit required to ride Camp Tamarancho. No parking on scout property.

Central Marin

Tamarancho Boy Scout Camp
Fairfax

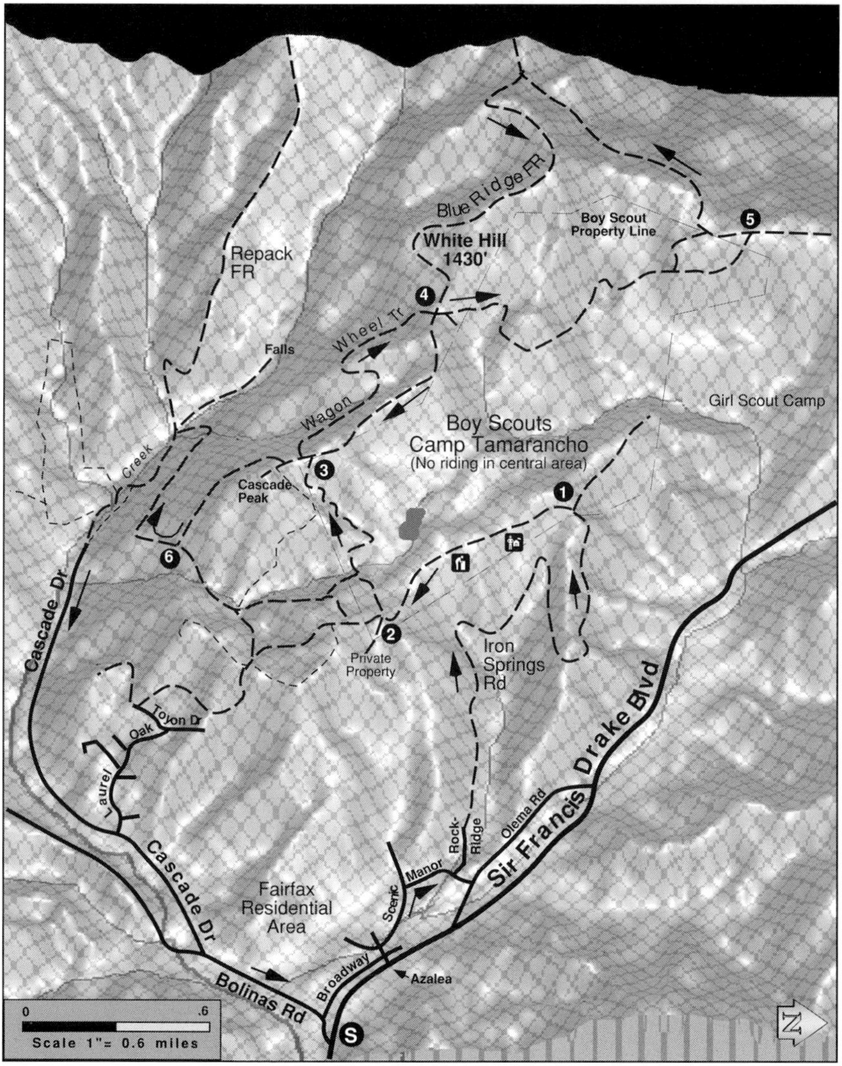

19 Deer Park - Pine Mountain - Repack

Distance: 11.0 miles ***Riding Time:*** 1.5-2 hours
Elevation Change: 1400' ***Difficulty:*** Strenuous
Technical Rating: 9 Rocky climb. Steep, rocky and rutted descent.
Steep, rutted and rocky fire roads dominate this ride, which includes Repack, where Marin's first mountain bike race was held. Unique geology and a pygmy forest make up the landscape. Bring sunscreen.

0.0 Start at Deer Park. The trail goes behind the school on the left, crosses a field and continues through a fire gate.

1.0 Junction ❶ at Five Corners. Take 2nd right to climb Shaver Grade.

1.6 Junction with Sky Oaks Rd. Go right down the road.

1.9 Junction ❷ near the Sky Oaks Ranger Station. At the parking area, go left, past the gate onto a fire road. Fifty feet in, the road splits; go straight. At **2.1** miles, you reach a T-junction; go right around the golf course (golf course will be on your left).

2.9 Golf course clubhouse at Bolinas-Fairfax Rd. When you reach the clubhouse go through the parking area to the main road, then head left and climb up the Bolinas-Fairfax Rd.

4.3 Hilltop, junction ❸ and parking area (1080'). Go right past a fire gate and onto the Pine Mtn FR. At **4.7** miles, the ride begins a technical steep climb. Green and blue serpentine rock compose most of the trail and also stunts much of the tree growth. This causes pockets of pygmy forest (mostly Sargent cypress) along the way.

5.9 Junction of San Geronimo Ridge Rd. Go right on the FR and watch for the next FR coming up on the right.

6.2 Junction ❹ at Repack FR is unsigned (1500'). Go right. About 100 yds. in, you'll pass a gate that marks the boundary between MMWD and Marin County Open Space. This is a steep, rocky and rutted, 2 mile descent. Be careful and have fun!

8.2 Cross the bridge at the bottom of Repack. The FR goes through Cascade Creek 4 times, so be ready to get wet. If the water is extremely high there is an alternate route to the left, just before the first stream crossing, which meets up at the gate (**9.0** miles).

9.0 Gate at entrance to Eliot Nature Preserve and end of Cascade Drive. Take Cascade Drive to Bolinas-Fairfax Rd. (**10.2** miles). Go right and in 100 yds., make a left on Porteous Ave and follow it to the end at Deer Park (**11.0** miles).

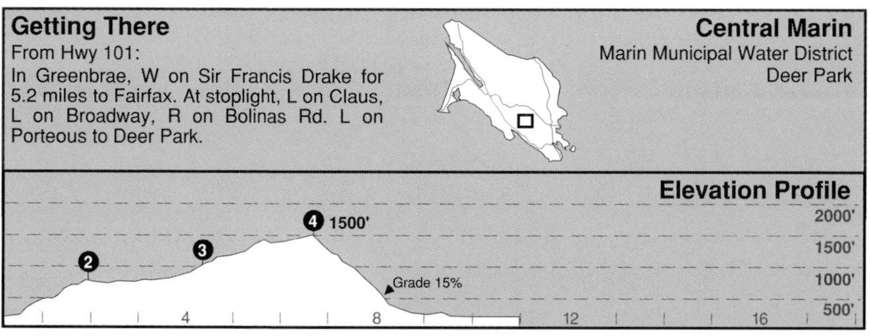

Getting There

From Hwy 101:

In Greenbrae, W on Sir Francis Drake for 5.2 miles to Fairfax. At stoplight, L on Claus, L on Broadway, R on Bolinas Rd. L on Porteous to Deer Park.

Central Marin

Marin Municipal Water District
Deer Park

Elevation Profile

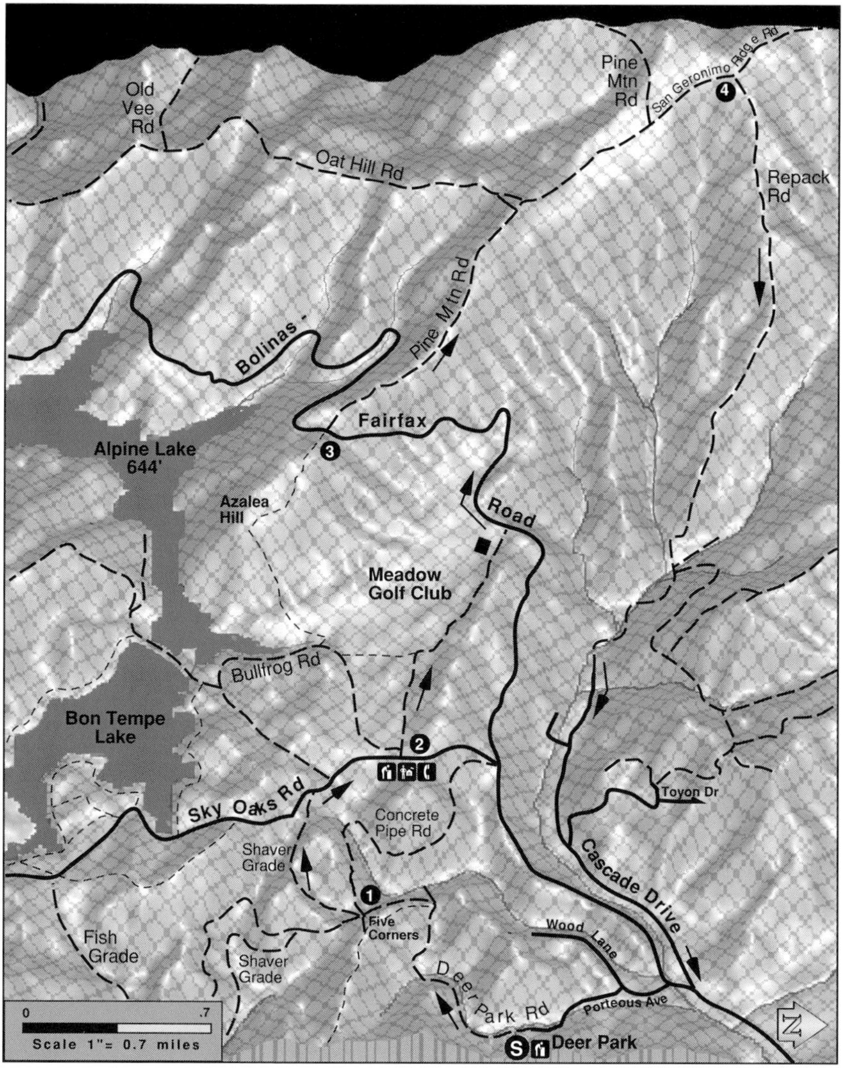

20A Deer Park to Stinson Beach

Distance: 46.7 miles ***Riding Time:*** 4-6 hours
Elevation Change: 5600' ***Difficulty:*** Extreme
Technical Rating: 9 Some rocky climbing, steep descents.
Tour Marin's best locations that range from the difficult to the sublime. Ascend to the top of Mt. Tam, and then descend steeply to Stinson Beach. Finish on a roller coaster ride down Bolinas Ridge.

0.0 Ride left of the school and through a fire gate. Follow Deer Park FR through oak-bay woodland. At **0.7** miles, stay left.

1.4 Five Corners. Take the second FR on the right, Shaver Grade.

2.0 Junction ❶ at top of Shaver. Go left on the paved Sky Oaks Rd.

3.5 Lagunitas parking lot. Ride up to the dam on the FR at the left end of the lot, then go right to circle the lake counter-clockwise.

4.7 Lakeview FR junction ❷ (800'). Go right to start the serious climb up Mt. Tam. At **5.5** miles, take Eldridge Grade uphill. Great views of the East Bay start to appear along this section. At 6.5 miles, there is a junction with Indian FT. Stay right to make the final ascent to the top.

9.0 Junction ❸ at the top of Eldridge Grade. Go left on the paved Ridgecrest Blvd to the East Peak lookout (**9.3** mi.). On weekends a snack shop is open, bring money to reload your fuel cells. Views of the ocean and SF. It's also a popular spot with tourists and locals alike. Ride back down Ridgecrest and follow it as it traverses the three peaks of Mt. Tam. A long descent marks where you need to start looking for the next junction, which is easily missed.

12.0 Junction ❹ of Rock Springs FR. Look for it on the right hand side of Ridgecrest Blvd across from a large gravel parking area. There's a tall wooden sign marking the trail. Go right on Rock Springs FR up a couple of steep climbs and drop into Portrero Meadows.

12.8 Junction with Laurel Dell FR. Go left. The FR rolls as it takes you to Laurel Dell, a serene glade with a creek running through it. Cross the creek at Laurel Dell to climb back up to Ridgecrest Blvd.

15.1 Junction ❺ with Ridgecrest Blvd (2000'). Go left and in about 100 yds., look for a fire gate on the right side. This is the Willow Camp trail that plummets towards Stinson Beach (once known as Willow Camp). The panoramic coastline and ocean views are fantastic. Out to sea, the Farallon Islands can be seen on clear days, but you'll have to stop to look because this is one of the steepest descents in all of Marin. (Continued on the next page).

Getting There

From Hwy 101:

In Greenbrae, W on Sir Francis Drake for 5.2 miles to Fairfax. At stoplight, L on Claus, L on Broadway, R on Bolinas Rd. L on Porteous to Deer Park.

Central Marin

Marin Municpal Water District
Deer Park

Elevation Profile
Note change in horizontal scale.
2000'
1500'
1000'
500'
Grade 18%
12
24
36
48

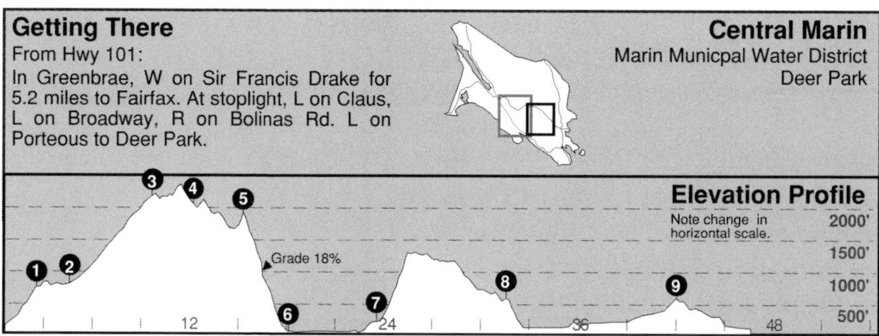

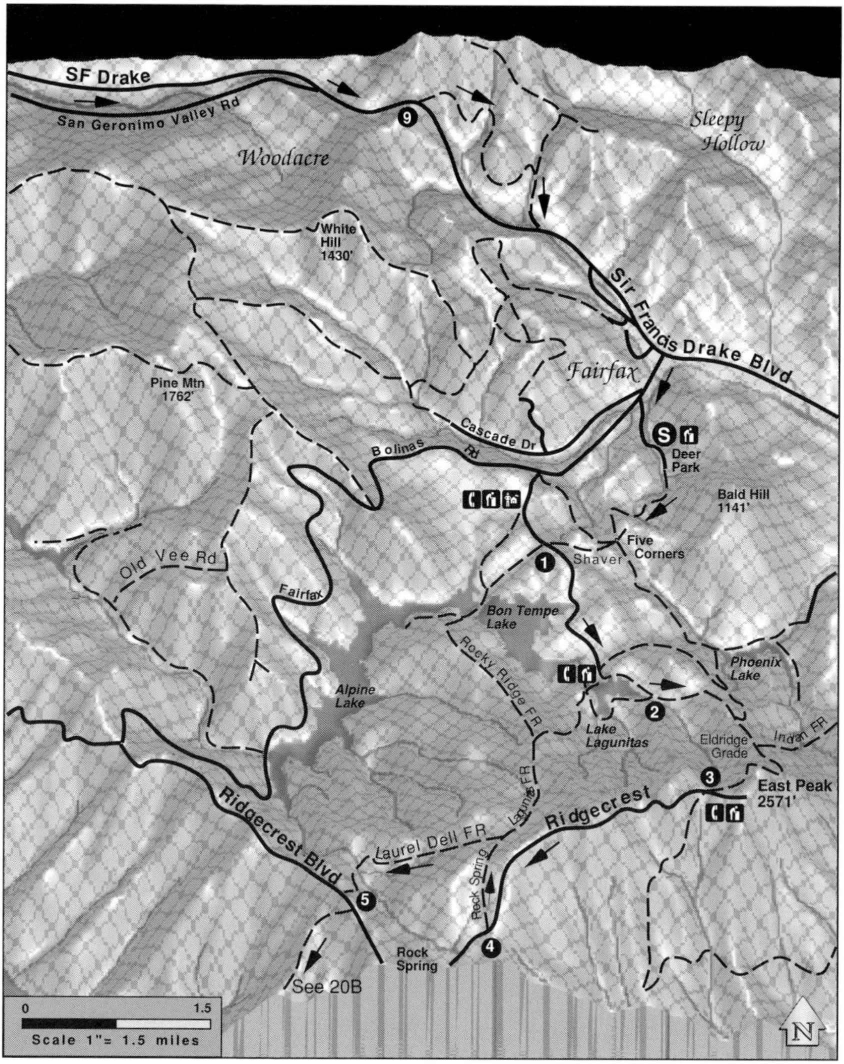

SF Drake
San Geronimo Valley Rd
Woodacre
Sleepy Hollow
White Hill 1430'
Sir Francis Drake Blvd
Fairfax
Pine Mtn 1762'
Cascade Dr
Bolinas Rd
S
Deer Park
Bald Hill 1141'
Five Corners
Shaver
Old Vee Rd
Fairfax
Bon Tempe Lake
Rocky Ridge FR
Phoenix Lake
Alpine Lake
Lake Lagunitas
Eldridge Grade
Indian FR
East Peak 2571'
Ridgecrest
Ridgecrest Blvd
Lagunitas FR
Laurel Dell FR
Rock Spring
Rock Spring
See 20B
0
1.5
Scale 1"= 1.5 miles
N

20B Deer Park to Stinson - Continued

15.1 Junction ❺ on Ridgecrest Blvd. Time to head downhill. Keep your weight back, and staff off your front brake in the turns!

17.0 Junction with FR. Go left and then take a right at the next FR junction to ride towards the end of a paved road.

17.4 Avenida Farallone. Go down the street, then left on Belvedere, right on Lincoln, right on Calle del Mar into town.

18.1 Junction ❻ with Hwy 1. You can't beat Stinson Beach for a rest stop. Stock up on water and food here. The ride now goes north (right) on Hwy 1, passing the Bolinas Rd. cut-off and Dogtown. After Dogtown, start to look for the next junction.

23.3 Junction ❼. Take McCurdy trail on right, across the highway from Olema Valley Trailhead. Go into the dirt parking area and look for the single track trail on your left. The trail rises up over a knoll before widening into an old FR. It's steep and can be hot and arduous.

25.2 Top of McCurdy, Bolinas Ridge (1450'). Go left on FR. Ride through redwood forest here along the top. In a couple of miles the FR descends and opens up to a swooping grassy ridge. The descent is fast and especially fun for dualies, who can glide over the ruts without decreasing speed. After 6.4 miles of downhill (**31.6** mi.), look for an old unsigned FR on the right as you make a swooping left turn.

31.6 Junction ❽. Go right onto the Jewell trail into Taylor Park.

32.6 Bikepath. Go right on bike path, past the campground and over an old bridge. When the river is deep, take SF Drake Hwy at the bridge.

36.5 The FR/trail deadends at Shafter Bridge and there's a small trail to the right that crosses the creek and climbs up the other side to the road. Take this road, Sir Francis Drake, east towards Fairfax. At **37.3** miles, Lagunitas Store may prove a welcome last respite before the final leg over White Hill.

42.1 Junction ❾ at the top of White Hill (use Map 20A). Cross the road when safe and take the FR on the left, which cuts off a dangerous White Hill descent next to cars. Stay left at the Y-junction at **42.5** miles. The FR narrows into a short single track that dips into a ravine before widening out to FR again. Take a right at the Y-junction at **43.5** miles to drop into Manor School. Go out of school and right onto road. Go left on Sir Francis Drake and ride back into Fairfax.

45.5 Stoplight in town. Go right, then quick left, then right again onto Bolinas Rd. Ride to Porteous Ave and take a left to ride back to your car at **46.7** miles. A long trek, but worth the effort!

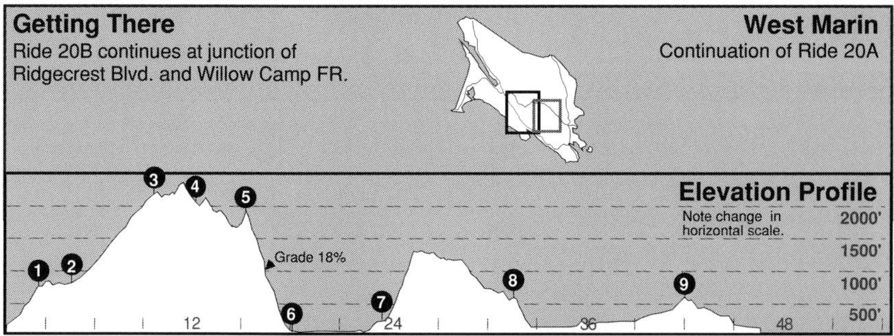

Getting There

Ride 20B continues at junction of Ridgecrest Blvd. and Willow Camp FR.

West Marin

Continuation of Ride 20A

Elevation Profile
Note change in horizontal scale.
2000'
1500'
1000'
500'
1
2
3
4
5
6
7
8
9
Grade 18%
12
24
36
48

Jewell Trail
8
Mt. Barnabe 1466'
Nicasio Valley Rd
Sir Francis Drake
See 20A
Bolinas Ridge FR
1
Five Brooks
Kent Lake
White Hill 1430'
Randall Trail
Pine Mtn 1762'
McCurdy Trail
Bolinas Ridge FR
Bolinas-Fairfax Rd
7
Alpine Lake
Ridgecrest
5
Willow Camp Trail
Pacific Ocean
Bolinas Lagoon
Stinson Beach
Bolinas
6
N
0
1.9
Scale 1"= 1.9 miles

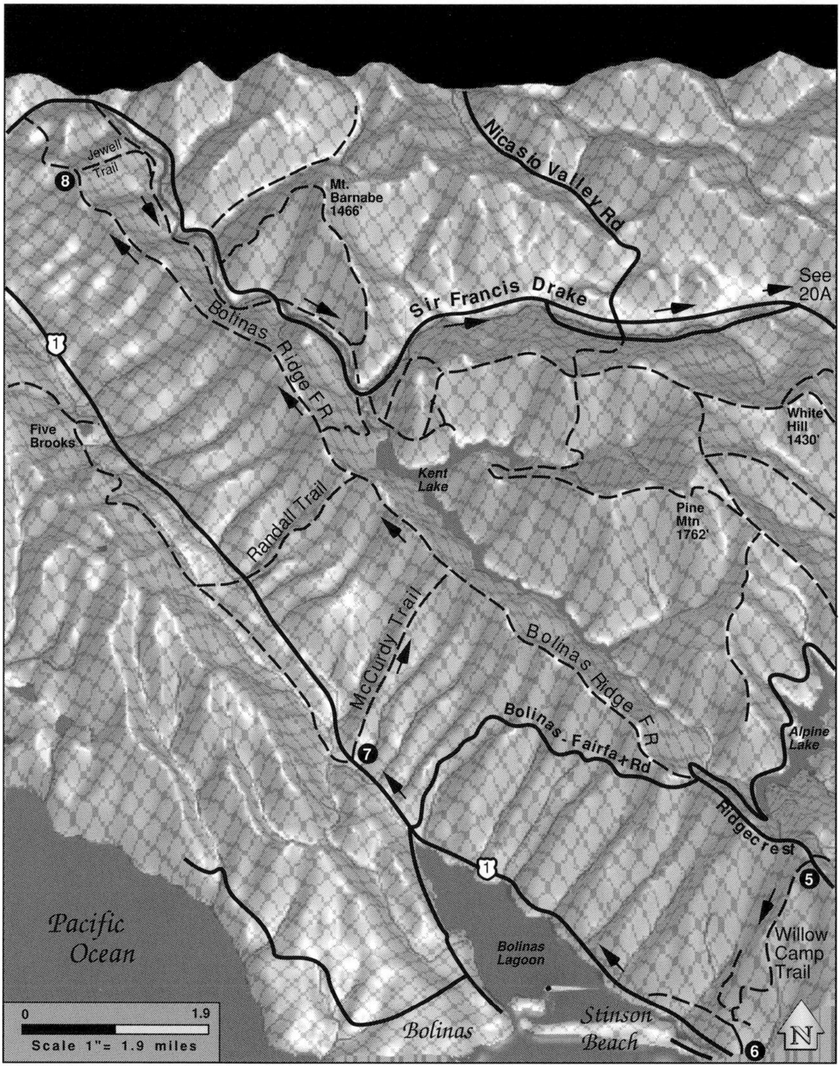

21 Sky Oaks - Lake Lagunitas Ride

Distance: 8.1 miles ***Riding Time:*** 1-1.5 hours
Elevation Change: 800' ***Difficulty:*** Easy to moderate
Technical Rating: 3 Mostly paved road and smooth FR.

A pleasant tour of the MMWD watershed area. The ride goes through meadows and around lakes, including idyllic Lake Lagunitas. Great outing for families with kids or beginning riders.

0.0 Start at the parking area just past the Sky Oaks Ranger Station and take Bullfrog FR west into Bon Tempe meadow. The FR skirts the left side of the meadow and then climbs up to an old quarry where rock was mined for Bon Tempe Dam. Look for bush rabbits and listen for frogs in the evening hours.

Lake Lagunitas

1.0 Junction ❶ and parking area. Go right through the gate and up the road to the Bon Tempe Dam. Cross the dam and turn right to travel down along Lake Alpine.

1.9 Junction ❷. The road ends at the Kent trailhead. Backtrack to continue the ride. Views of two lakes. Go right off the dam.

3.2 Junction with Sky Oaks Rd. Go right to climb up and over a saddle towards another arm of Bon Tempe Lake. Continue on the paved road around the lake through another meadow towards Mt. Tam. At **4.5** mi., veer right towards the Lake Lagunitas parking lot.

4.6 Junction ❸ and parking lot. Take the road on the left side of the parking area up to the dam. Once at the dam ride counter-clockwise around the lake. This is one of the most beautiful spots in all of Marin. The lake is a serene yet vibrant home for many species of plants and animals. It is sheltered by Mt. Tam's magnificent slopes. At **4.9** mi., stay left to continue along the lake shore. There are three stream crossings that you can either ride through or navigate over bridges.

5.8 Junction with Lakeview FR (816'). Turn left to go back towards the dam. The FR ends in a single track that takes you down some stairs back to the dam. Head back to the parking area.

6.5 Junction ❸ again. Ride back along Sky Oaks Rd., staying on the paved road all the way to the ranger station parking area at **8.1** miles.

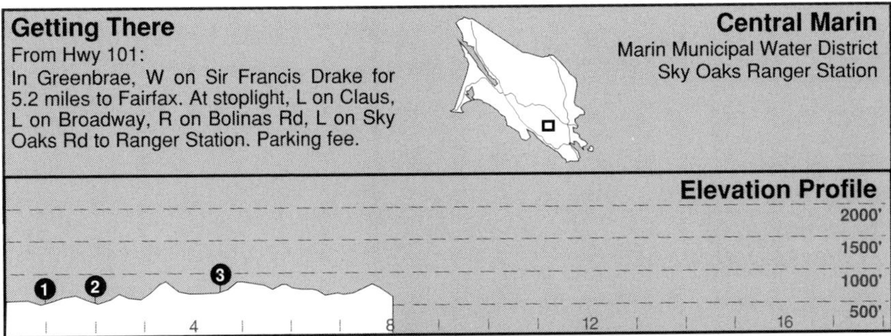

Getting There

From Hwy 101:

In Greenbrae, W on Sir Francis Drake for 5.2 miles to Fairfax. At stoplight, L on Claus, L on Broadway, R on Bolinas Rd, L on Sky Oaks Rd to Ranger Station. Parking fee.

Central Marin

Marin Municipal Water District
Sky Oaks Ranger Station

Elevation Profile

2000'
1500'
1000'
500'
4
8
12
16

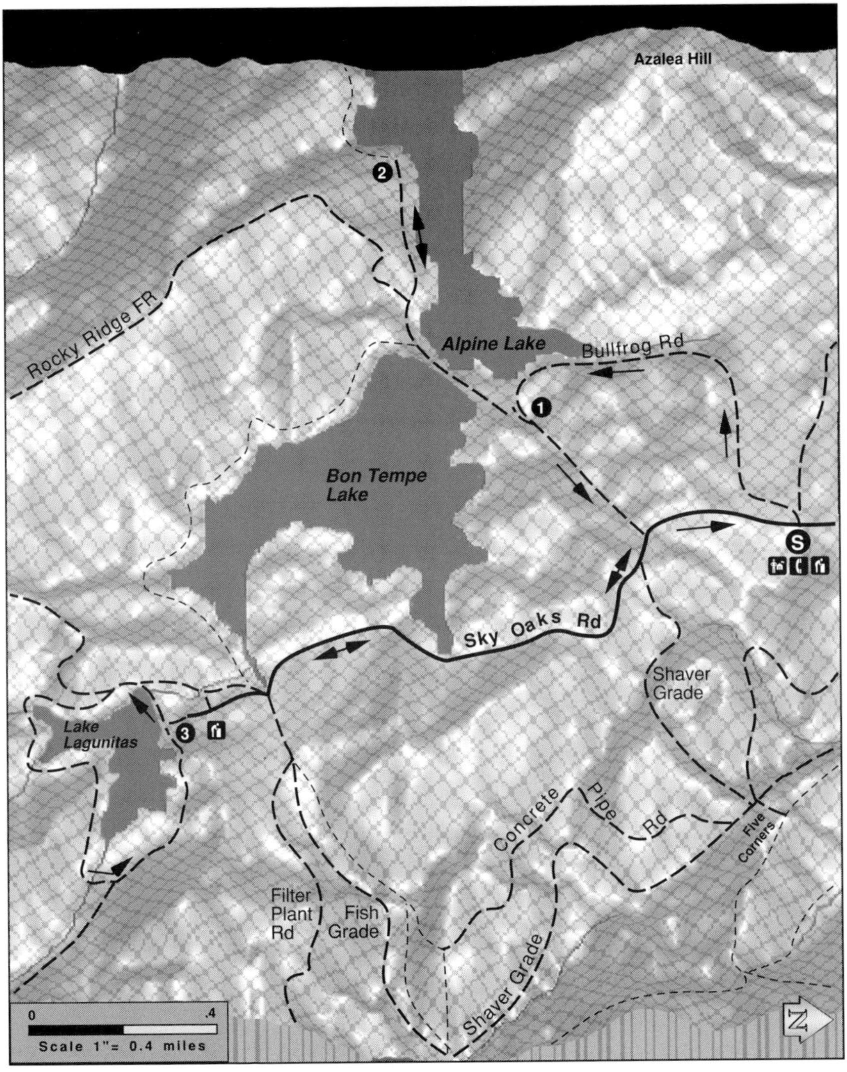

Azalea Hill
Rocky Ridge FR
Alpine Lake
Bullfrog Rd
Bon Tempe Lake
Sky Oaks Rd
Lake Lagunitas
Shaver Grade
Concrete Pipe Rd
Five Corners
Filter Plant Rd
Fish Grade
Shaver Grade
S
0
.4
Scale 1"= 0.4 miles
N

22 Pine Mountain Loop

Distance: 13.4 miles ***Riding Time:*** 2-2.5 hours
Elevation Change: 2900' ***Difficulty:*** Strenuous
Technical Rating: 8 Extremely rocky, rutted and steep.

Marin's most remote ride. Tough, rocky and steep fire roads take you through Sargent cypress and chaparral on the ridge tops. Redwoods, fir and bay provide some shade in the lakeside canyons.

0.0 Start from parking area on Bolinas Rd. and ride up Pine Mtn. FR, a steep rocky grind. Pass the junction of Oat Hill FR at **1.1** miles.

1.6 Junction ❶ of Pine Mtn. FR and San Geronimo Ridge FR. Go left on Pine Mtn. FR and climb to the summit of Pine Mtn. at **2.4** mile (1762'). A small trail from the FR leads to the actual summit and a rocky outcropping sheltered from the wind by shrubs. Continue on along the ridge.

3.6 Knoll. Bolinas Ridge to the west, Kent Lake below in the canyon, Tomales Bay to the north and Mt. Tam to the south are highlights of the view. (marker on knoll, GS21). This knoll is also a fine place to see hawks from above as they float on thermals below.

The fabled Paradigm trail was built near here by bikers. The trail caused major controversy with the water district. It was permantly closed by MMWD at a cost of more than $25,000.

5.3 Leave the ridge top and descend into the forest of the Kent Lake drainage; the trail gets steep so be careful.

5.7 Unsigned T-junction. Go right. The left trail deadends. The trail meanders along Kent Lake, through riparian habitat and across streams, then climbs back out of the other side of the Kent Lake drainage basin.

8.9 Four-way junction ❷. Green Mtn. lies uphill to the left. Take a right onto San Geronimo Ridge FR. At **9.9** miles, you pass through a meadow with trails coming in from the left. Stay right to climb back to a rocky ridge top.

11.4 Repack FR on the left (1480'). Continue straight, into a short rocky, technical descent.

11.8 Junction of Pine Mtn. FR and San Geronimo Ridge FR. Go straight to retrace your ride back to the parking area. The steep rocky descent is the last of the ride.

13.4 Back at the parking area.

Getting There

From Hwy 101:
In Greenbrae, W on Sir Francis Drake for 5.2 miles to Fairfax. At stoplight, L on Claus, L on Broadway, R on Bolinas Rd. for 3.8 miles to parking area at top of hill.

Central Marin

Marin Municipal Water District
Pine Mountain

Elevation Profile

Pine Mountain
2000'
1500'
1000'
500'
4
8
12
16

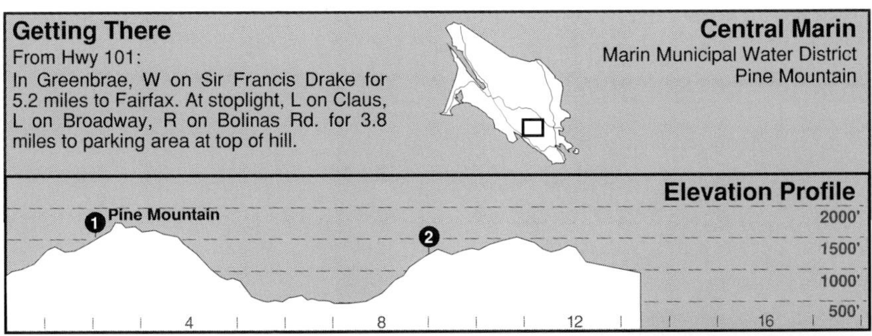

Bolinas Ridge FR
Kent Lake
Kent Lake
Pine Mtn Rd
Green Hill
1418'
Pine Mtn
1762'
Old
Vee
Rd
San Geronimo Ridge Rd
Carson
Falls
Oat Hill Rd
Repack
FR
Pine
Mtn.
Rd.
Fairfax -
Bolinas
Rd
Azalea Hill
White Hill
1430'
Cascade
Falls
Tamarancho
Boy Scout Camp
0
.8
Scale 1"= 0.8 miles
N

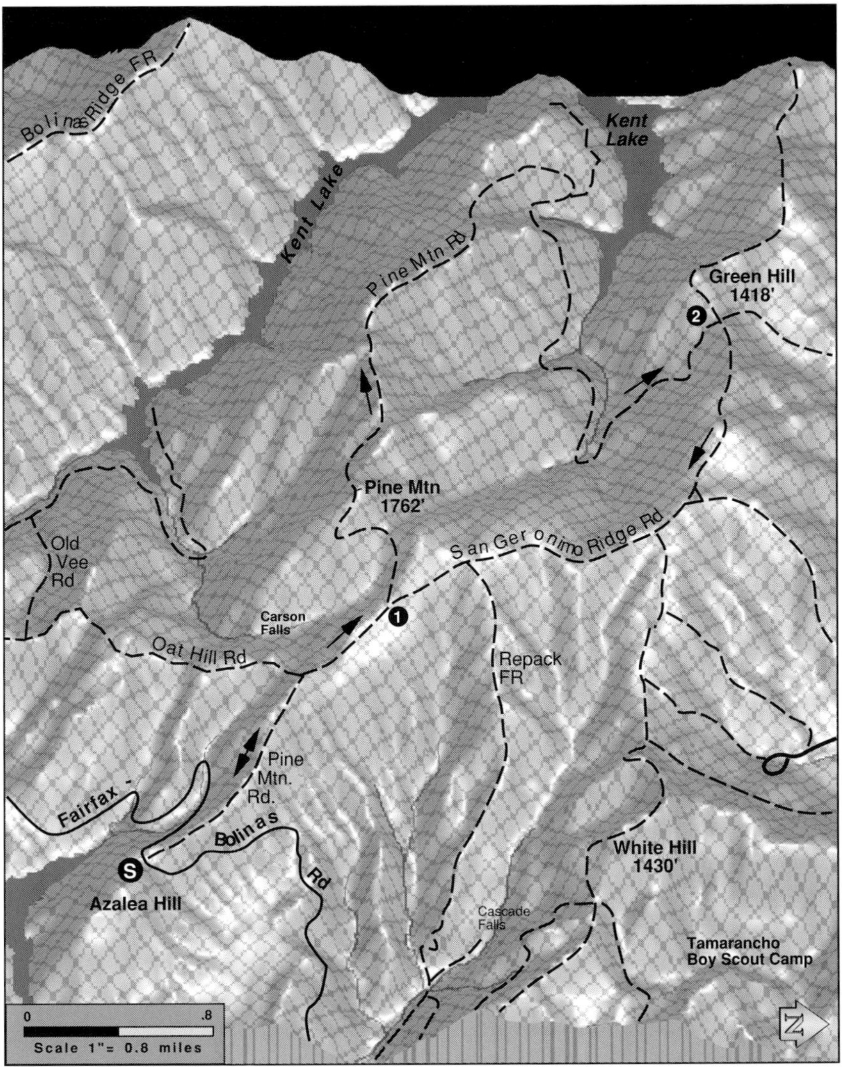

23 Pine Mountain - Old Vee FR

Distance: 13.9 miles ***Riding Time:*** 2-2.5 hours
Elevation Change: 1300' ***Difficulty:*** Moderate
Technical Rating: 7 Rocky and rutted climbs and descents.

Rugged terrain, lakeside setting and a final road burn makes this an excellent choice for the intermediate rider. Old Vee is a seldom used trail, offering a good chance to see animal life and get a remote feeling.

0.0 Ride out Pine Mtn. Rd. The FR is rocky and towards the end of the first mile it climbs one of the steepest, most technical uphill fire roads in all of Marin. Advanced riders may be able to "clean" this section, but the rest of us have to get off and hike-a-bike.

1.1 Junction ❶ of Oat Hill FR (1400'). Go left down Oat Hill FR, which loosely follows a southern ridge. There are great views to the west and east as you follow this ridge up and down. The East Bay can be seen in the distance as you round the east side of the ridge and Mt. Tam dominates the landscape to the south.

2.9 Junction ❷ of Old Vee FR (1250'). Take Old Vee right to drop off the west side of the ridge. This FR has rocks and is rutted, and it gets steep towards the end. Watch your speed, especially coming into blind turns that sharpen at the end and may cause you to fly off the trail. There isn't much traffic out here, so we don't recommend that you ride alone.

4.0 Junction ❸ of Alpine-Kent Pump Rd. Go right. At the pump station (**5.4** mi.), take the first right, for a moderate climb. The road deadends at **5.7** miles at an old hunting camp in a redwood grove. In winter, there are two waterfalls, about 200 yds. and 800 yds. upstream. To explore further, look for a redwood bridge in the grove.

7.4 Junction ❸ again. Continue on the FR, which is flat and fast, going through a deep canyon covered by a canopy of mature trees including Douglas fir, oak, and bay.

9.4 Fork in road. Veer left to rise towards the top of the dam.

9.7 Junction ❹ at Alpine Dam and Bolinas-Fairfax Rd. Ride left onto the paved Bolinas-Fairfax Rd. The road borders the lake for about one-half mile, then heads inland. There is occasional traffic out here, sometimes going too fast and cutting corners. With the windy road and short sightlines, keep to the right of the road and stay alert. At **12.9** miles, you hit the last steady climb up to the saddle and parking lot at **13.9** miles.

Getting There

From Hwy 101:
In Greenbrae, W on Sir Francis Drake for 5.2 miles to Fairfax. At stoplight, L on Claus, L on Broadway, R on Bolinas Rd. for 3.8 miles to parking area at top of hill.

Central Marin

Marin Municipal Water District
Pine Mountain

Elevation Profile
1
2
3
4
2000'
1500'
1000'
500'
4
8
12
16

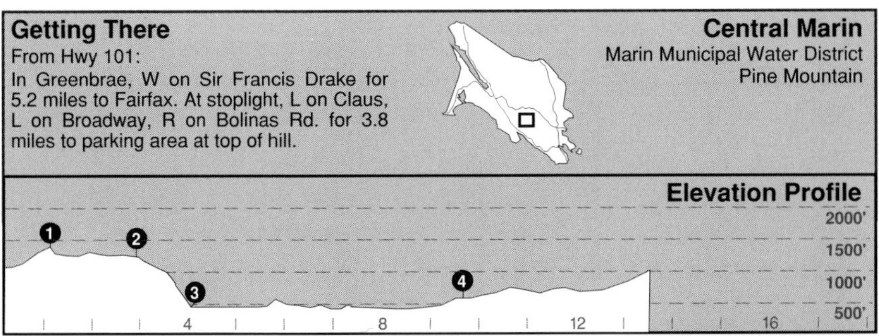

Bolinas FR
Kent Lake
3
Old Vee Rd
Alpine - Kent Pump Rd
2
Oat Hill Rd
Carson Falls
1
4
Oat Hill 1200'
Pine Mtn Rd
Bolinas
Fairfax
Rd
Alpine Lake
S
Azalea Hill
0
.6
Scale 1"= 0.6 miles
N

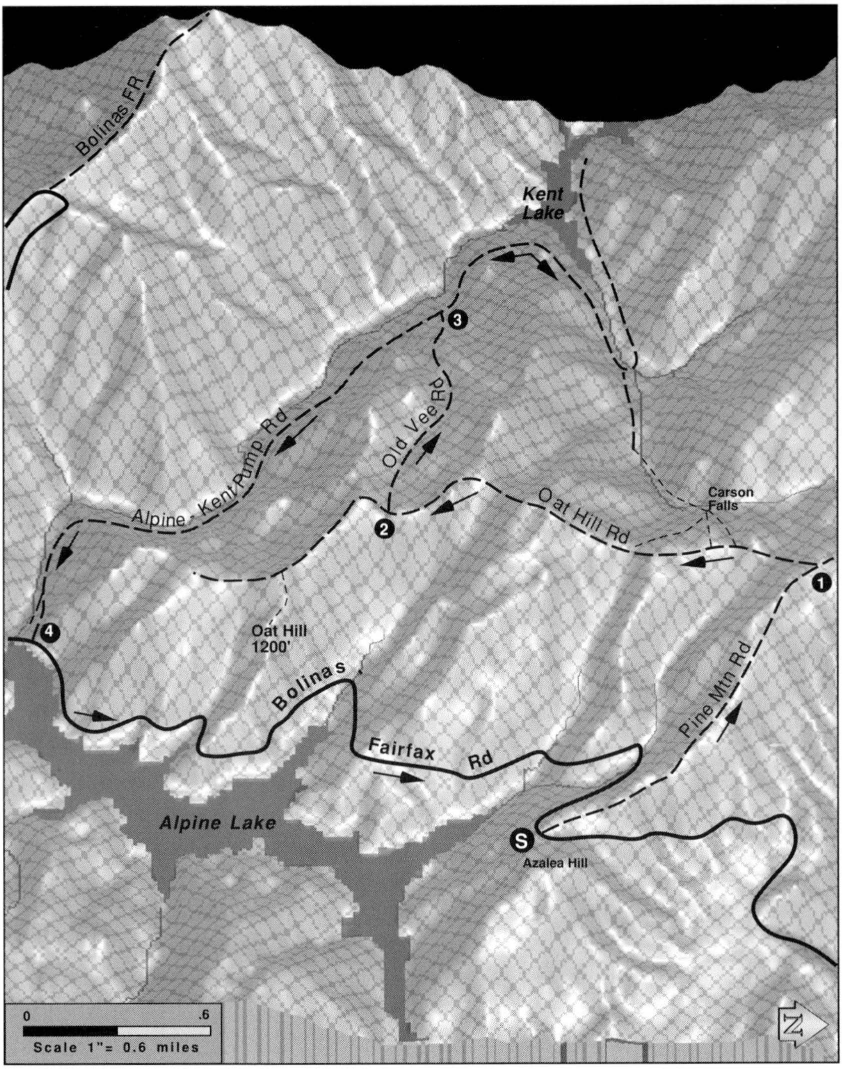

24 Shoreline Trail to China Camp Village

Distance: 8.2 miles *Riding Time:* 1.5-2 hours
Elevation Change: 250' *Difficulty:* Easy
Technical Rating: 3 Wide and winding single track, some ruts.

This ride is a mostly flat, single track romp in the popular China Camp State Park. It's great for beginners wanting to venture out onto single track and intermediate riders looking for a cruise. Mostly shady.

0.0 From the parking area along the road, ride onto the Shoreline trail to the right of the campground kiosk. This wide, single track is designed for multi-use and you may encounter others enjoying the natural scenery. At **0.1** miles, continue left on Shoreline.

0.2 Parking area. Cross the parking area and continue on Shoreline.

1.0 Junction ❶ with Back Ranch FT. Go straight on the Shoreline trail that winds along the meadows and hillsides bordering San Pablo Bay.

2.6 The trail ends in a parking area for Miwok Meadows Group Area. Ride out of the parking area on the dirt road. At **2.9** miles, Shoreline resumes on the right side of the road.

4.7 Junction ❷. Go left to switchback down to the ranger station. There, cross the paved road to continue on Shoreline Trail.

5.2 Junction ❸. Take the Village trail left down into a lush canyon, cross over North San Pedro Road to enter China Camp Historic Village at **5.5** miles. This used to be a Chinese fishing village in the late 1800s. The immigrants netted shrimp from the waters of the bay to sell locally and in China. Restrictions on nets and changes in the market led to the decline and eventual abandonment of shrimp fishing. Walk around to check out the historic buildings. There is a small museum here and a snack bar open on weekends.

Keep China Camp Open

China Camp State Park is the only state park in Marin to allow riding on single track trails. It is an unofficial test to see if bikers, hikers and equestrians can jointly use single track trails. You can help by being friendly and courteous, riding in control and obeying the rules. We need to demonstrate that the overwhelming number of bikers are responsible users of the China Camp state park system.

To continue the ride, head back up to the main road (**5.8** mi.). Here, you have two options; return on the Shoreline trail (another 5.2 mi.) or take North San Pedro Rd. (another 2.4 mi.) back to the start.

Getting There

From Hwy 101:

In San Rafael, E on North San Pedro Rd for 3.1 miles to Back Ranch Campground. Park along road.

Central Marin

China Camp State Park
Campground Entrance

Elevation Profile
2000'
1500'
1000'
500'
4
8
12
16
1
2

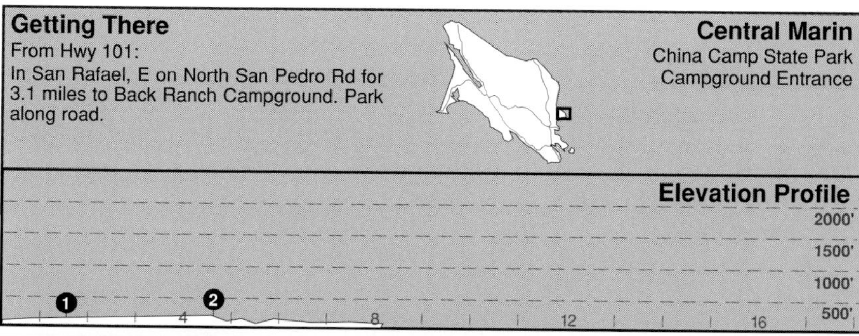

San Pedro Mtn 1058'
Nike Radar Site
Bay Hills Dr
Bay View Trail
North San Pedro Road
Back Ranch FT
Ridge Fire Trail
Bay View Trail
Back Ranch
Shoreline Tr
Group Area
Miwok Meadows
Turtle Back Island
Jakes Island
Miwok FT
Oak Ridge Trail
McNear Fire Trail
Oak Ridge Trail
Shoreline Tr
San Francisco Bay
Biscayne Drive
Peacock Gap Golf Course
China Camp Historic Village
0
.5
Scale 1"= 0.5 miles

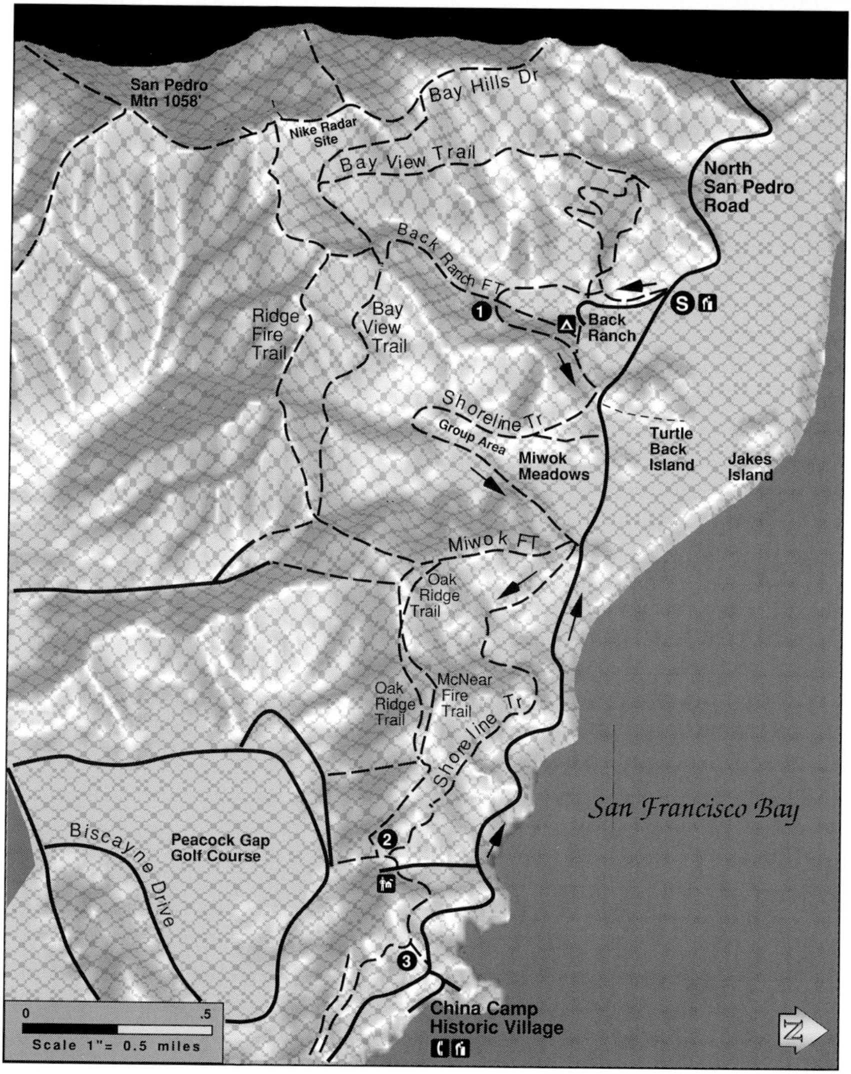

25 Bay View - Shoreline Trails

Distance: 10.3 miles ***Riding Time:*** 1-1.5 hours
Elevation Change: 700' ***Difficulty:*** Easy to moderate
Technical Rating: 5 Some narrow sections of trail and tricky turns.
A great single track ride that winds through oak-bay woodland along the hills bordering San Pablo Bay. The park has adopted a mult-iuse policy for it's single track that makes it very popular with cyclists.

0.0 Park anywhere along the road near Back Ranch Meadows campground. Start at the entrance to the campground and get on the single track to the right of the kiosk behind the water fountain. At **0.1** miles, the trail Y's, go right up Bay View trail.

0.5 Junction ❶ with Powerline FR. Go right and in about 25', make a left to return to the single track. At **1.0** mile, the trail meets back up with Powerline FT. Make a hard left (U-turn) to climb the single track. A picnic bench sits about halfway up for a nice rest stop. Just past the bench you'll find views of San Pablo Bay and Jakes Island.

At **2.0** miles, Bay Hills trail comes in from right, this is the highest point of your climb (600'). Continue on Bay View trail.

2.4 Junction ❷ of Back Ranch FR and Bay View. Go left down FR, in about 100 yds., take the single track on your right. The ride now consists of a series of swooping, downhill stretches. Watch for traffic!

3.7 Junction ❸. Go left on the Ridge Fire Road.

4.0 Junction of Ridge FR and Miwok FR. Go left down the FR and in about 50' take Oak Ridge trail (single track) on the right. At **4.3** miles, the trail crosses over Miwok Fire trail. At **4.7** miles, cross the Miwok FT again and switchback down the Oak Ridge trail.

5.2 Junction ❹ of Oak Ridge and Peacock Gap trail. Go left, in about 0.1 mile, veer left onto Shoreline trail, which is a gently rolling trail that heads all the way back to the start.

Option: Head right for 0.8 mile to visit historic China Camp Village.

7.0 Junction of Shoreline trail. Go left on FR in towards the Miwok Meadows group picnic area and catch trail at far end of parking lot. At **7.9** miles, veer left at fork in trail. At **8.2** miles, the trail hits North San Pedro Rd, but continue on the Shoreline trail to the left.

8.4 Three-way junction ❺. Keep left and stay on the Shoreline trail which circles around the canyon.

10.3 Back at the parking area.

Getting There

From Hwy 101:
In San Rafael, E on North San Pedro Rd for 3.1 miles to Back Ranch Campground. Park along road.

Central Marin

China Camp State Park
Campground Entrance

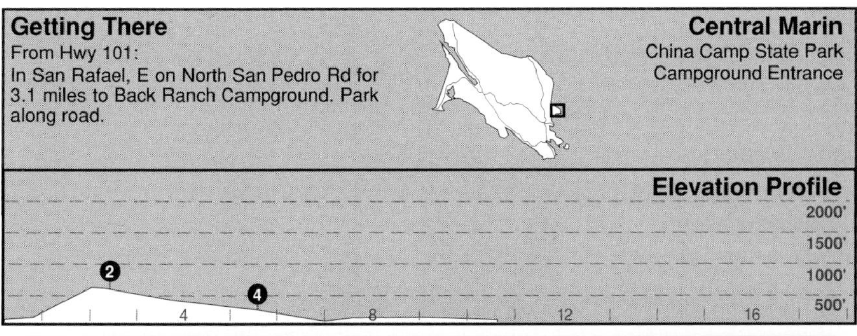

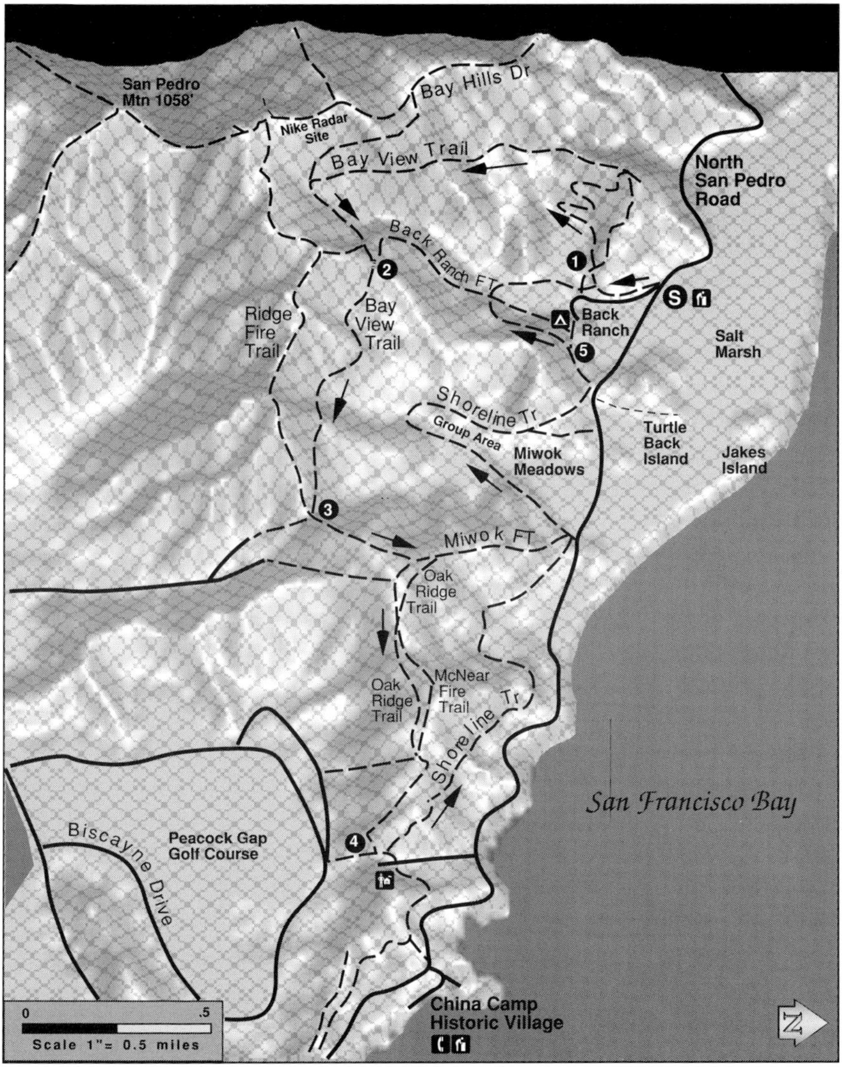

26 Bay Hills - Ridge FR - Bay View Trail

Distance: 11.5 miles ***Riding Time:*** 1.5-2 hours
Elevation Change: 1500' ***Difficulty:*** Moderate to strenuous
Technical Rating: 8 Steep descents, some tough uphill sections.
Explore the old Nike radar site and enjoy the sweeping SF bay views. This is the most difficult of the three China Camp rides as it climbs up to explore the ridge and multiple trails behind China Camp.

0.0 Take the Shoreline trail next to the kiosk in towards the canyon. Veer right at **0.1** mi. onto the Bay View trail. At **0.5** miles, cross the Powerline FR by going right, then left back to the single track.

1.1 Junction. Take the hairpin left to continue up Bay View trail. The climb up is fairly gradual through oak woodlands.

2.0 Junction ❶ with Bay Hills spur. Go right onto the switchback trail to contour around and meet Bayhills Dr., a paved road.

2.6 Junction with Bayhills Dr. Go left to grind up this steep road to the Nike radar site at **3.1** miles (900') on San Rafael open space (once owned by Frank Sinatra). Views of San Rafael, Mt. Tam and SF Bay. After a view stop, continue along the paved road. The city lands have numerous, unmarked, small trails that parallel the ridge roads.

3.3 Junction ❷ with Ridge FR. **Option**: Continue on the paved road to explore the ridgetop. Otherwise, go left on Ridge FR. This drops you back towards San Pablo Bay and onto another ridge. The fire road follows the ridge's steep descents and ascents to knolls, so you do some technical interval-style work along the way. Go past the FR on the right at **3.6** miles and past the FR on the left at **3.9** miles. At **4.6** miles, continue past a big, broad junction and stay on the fire road.

5.0 Junction ❸ of Miwok FR (400'). Go left down the steep FR. Watch out for loose dirt down towards the marsh.

5.5 Junction. Go right and then take another quick right onto Shoreline trail. At **6.8** miles, veer right at Y-junction, and then in about 100 yds., stay right again to catch Oak Ridge trail as it winds up the hill. The trail crosses the Ridge FR twice before ending at Miwok FR.

8.0 Junction ❸ again. Go left up the road and in about 100', catch Ridge FR on the right. Meet the big junction at **8.3** mi. This time take the Bay View single track to the right.

9.2 Back Ranch Meadows Fire Trail. Head up the trail 100', then take Bay View again on the right by the power line. Follow this back to the start at **11.5** miles.

Getting There

From Hwy 101:
In San Rafael, E on North San Pedro Rd for 3.1 miles to Back Ranch Campground. Park along road.

Central Marin

China Camp State Park
Campground Entrance

Elevation Profile

2000'
1500'
1000'
500'
4
8
12
16

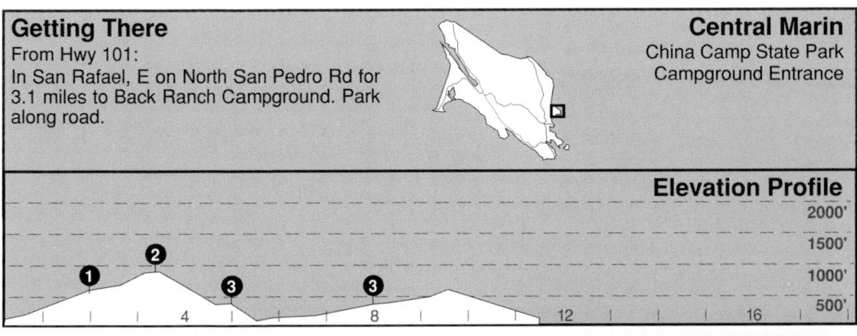

San Pedro Mtn 1058'
Nike Radar Site
Bay Hills Dr
Bay View Trail
Back Ranch FT
North San Pedro Road
Back Ranch
Ridge Fire Trail
Bay View Trail
Shoreline Tr
Group Area
Miwok Meadows
Turtle Back Island
Jakes Island
Miwok FT
Oak Ridge Trail
Oak Ridge Trail
McNear Fire Trail
Shoreline Tr
San Francisco Bay
Biscayne Drive
Peacock Gap Golf Course
China Camp Historic Village
0
.5
Scale 1" = 0.5 miles
N

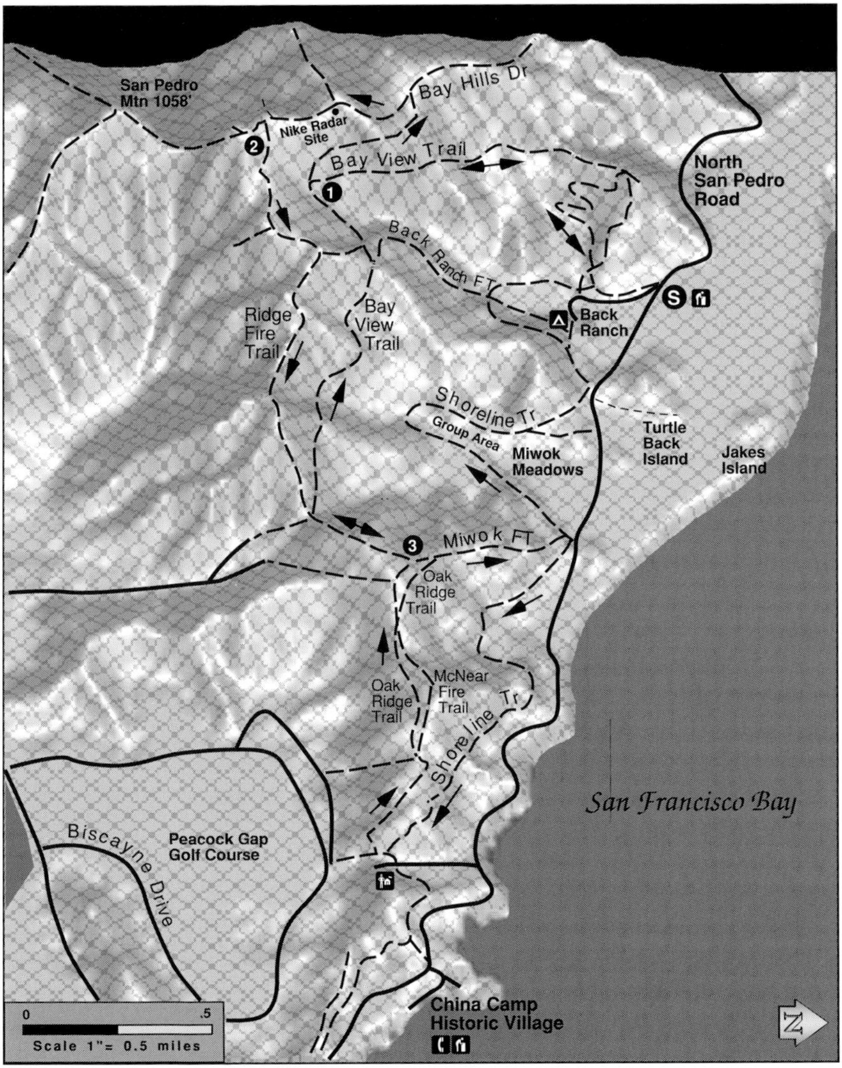

27 Loma Alta Peak Loop

Distance: 6.0 miles ***Riding Time:*** 1-1.5 hours
Elevation Change: 1200' ***Difficulty:*** Moderate
Technical Rating: 7 Some steep climbs and descents.
This short, peak-bag ride above the town of Fairfax, gives you a taste of the country while still close to town. On your way you explore two hidden valleys and part of a long-abandoned railroad grade.

0.0 Ride through the gate into open space past a FR on the left (**0.2** mi.) Stay on the road as it follows a forested creek drainage up the hill. This section of FR was part of a railroad line built in 1875, that went from Sausalito to West Marin via a tunnel through White Hill.

0.6 Junction ❶ and water tanks. Take the Smith Ridge FR that goes around the water tanks and up the hill past a gate.

2.0 Junction ❷ with Gunshot FR on your left. Continue uphill.

2.5 Saddle and fence at Loma Alta (1345'). Sweeping views of Marin. In the future, the MCOSD hopes to acquire easements that will allow us to continue through the gate and out the ridge to Roys Redwoods in San Geronimo or over Loma Alta Peak and down into Lucas Valley. For now, turn around and head back the way you came.

3.0 Junction ❷. Go right on Gunshot FR to plunge into the valley.

3.8 Junction ❸ with the old railroad line. Go left along the forgotten line. At **4.1** miles, there's a Y-junction, go left and down into a bowl. On the left is a small ravine with an unusually large (for here) waterfall. In the rainy season, this can be spectacular, but also very muddy. The road narrows and becomes overgrown at **4.3** miles. Follow the trail into another small wooded ravine and back up onto the flat trail that travels around the contour of the hill to take you over to the next valley where the ride started.

Winter Waterfall

4.7 Junction of FR. Stay left on FR to continue your traverse.

5.1 Y-junction. Stay left to ride along this contour. The FR again narrows into an unmaintained trail with some fun obstacles.

5.7 T-junction. Go right to turn into creek basin. The trail meets up with Glen FR in 0.1 mi. Stay right to go back to the car at **6.0** miles.

Getting There

From Hwy 101:

In Greenbrae, W on Sir Francis Drake for 6.6 miles to the outskirts of Fairfax. R on Glen Drive, past White Hill School to the end of the street.

Central Marin

Marin County Open Space

Loma Alta

Elevation Profile

2000'
1500'
1000'
500'
Grade 19%
1
2
3
4
8
12
16

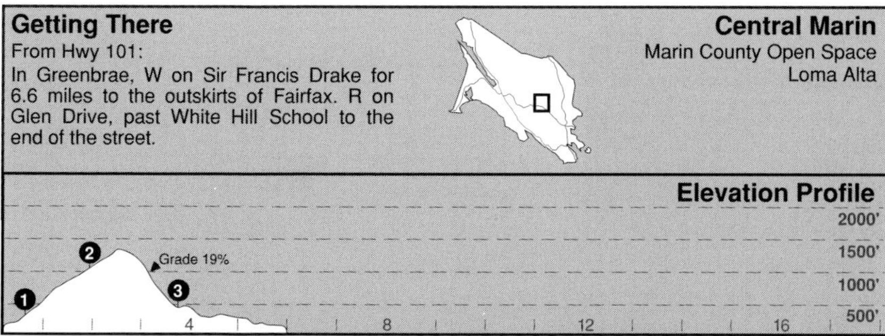

Loma Alta
1592'
Private
Private
Gunshot FR
Smith Ridge FR
Sleepy Hollow
Sir Francis Drake Blvd
Tanks
Private
1
2
3
Private
Baywood Canyon
Pipeline FR
S
White Hill School
Fairfax
0
.5
Scale 1"= 0.5 miles
N

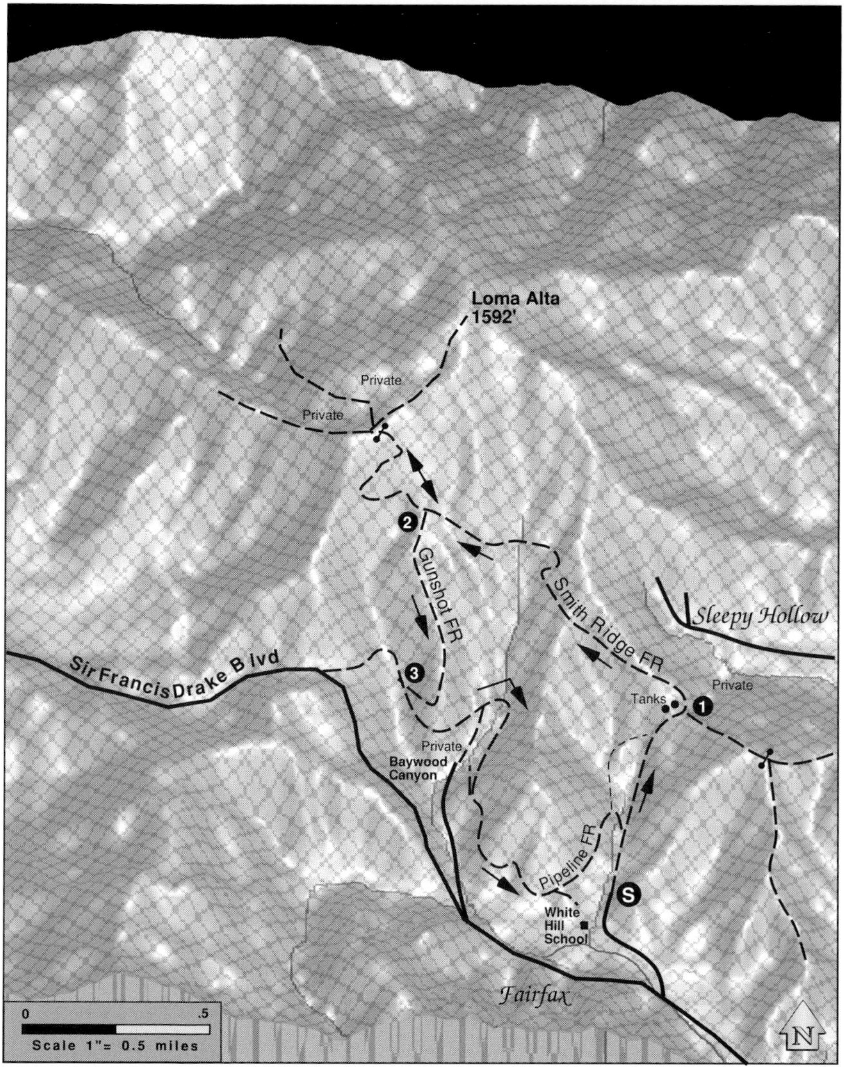

28 Ridge Trail to Mt. Barnabe

Distance: 7.4 miles ***Riding Time:*** 1.5-2 hours
Elevation Change: 1400' ***Difficulty:*** Moderate
Technical Rating: 8 Hairy fire road descent.
This ride in SP Taylor State Park makes a steep climb to bag Mt. Barnabe. Views of Tomales Bay, Point Reyes and west Marin. Change in ecosystems is dramatic - redwood forest to open grassland hillsides.

0.0 Start at the main entrance to Samuel P. Taylor State Park. Ride into park past kiosk and bear left over a bridge. Turn left again and follow signs towards group picnic ground. Continue on this former railroad bed, now the Hiking and Riding Trail as it parallels the creek, then crosses over Sir Francis Drake on a small bridge.

1.6 Junction ❶. Take the Barnabe Peak Ridge trail to the left at the signpost. The trail climbs in steep, terraced sections winding out of the trees into the open grassland towards the summit.

3.6 Mt. Barnabe and Junction ❷ at 1466'. Head up to the fire lookout for spectacular views of uninterrupted wilderness and distant peaks: Tomales Bay to the west, Mt. Diablo in Contra Costa County to the east, and Mt. St. Helena in the north. Go right down Barnabe trail as you come off the peak, a steep tricky fire road descent with off-camber corners. You'll pass by Bills trail to Devils Gulch on the right at **3.8** miles.

4.8 Junction ❸. Madrone picnic area is to the left. This is a quick way back. This ride continues to the right towards Devils Gulch.

4.9 Junction ❹ (440'). Taylors Grave (surrounded by a white picket fence) lies on a knoll directly ahead . Continue right towards Devils Gulch, ford a small creek and head up and over a short steep hill.

5.7 Junction ❺. T-junction of Bills trail and Devils Gulch trail. Go left to cross the bridge, then up to the paved road, Devils Gulch trail. Go left again and zip down to Sir Francis Drake Hwy.

5.9 Junction ❻ with Sir Francis Drake Hwy. Go right and carefully ride along the highway (towards Olema) for 0.3 mi. Cross the green bridge and head left to ride back along the Hiking and Riding trail. The first papermill on the west coast was built near the bridge in the 1870s. Back in the picnic area, look for a billboard that displays some great historical photos of the papermill, railroad and Camp Taylor.

7.3 Junction and Bridge. Cross the bridge and take the paved road back to the park headquarters (**7.4** miles).

Getting There

From Hwy 101:

In Greenbrae, W on Sir Francis Drake for 15.6 miles to the main entrance to Samuel P. Taylor State Park. Entrance fee.

Central Marin

Samuel P. Taylor State Park
Main Entrance

Elevation Profile

2 Mt. Barnabe
Grade 26%
3
1
2000'
1500'
1000'
500'
4
8
12
16

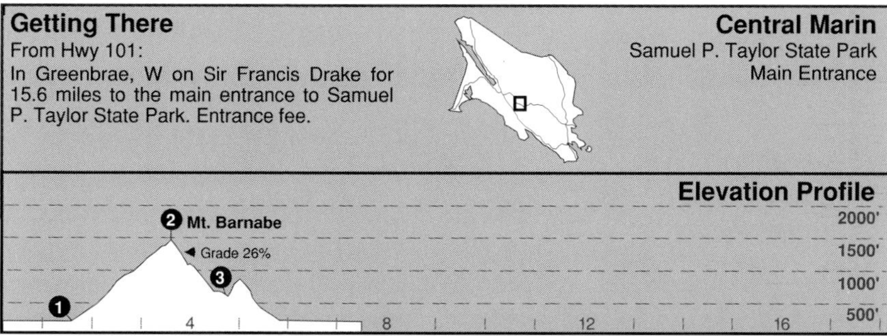

Deer Point
680'
Devils Gulch Trail
Bills Trail
Barnabe Trail
Barnabe Peak
1466'
2
5
6
4
Grave
3
Riding & Hiking Trail
Ridge Trail
Samuel P. Taylor State Park
Madrone Group Area
Main Entrance
S
Riding & Hiking Trail
Sir Francis Drake Hwy
1
Pioneer Tree Trail
0
.5
Scale 1"= 0.5 miles
N

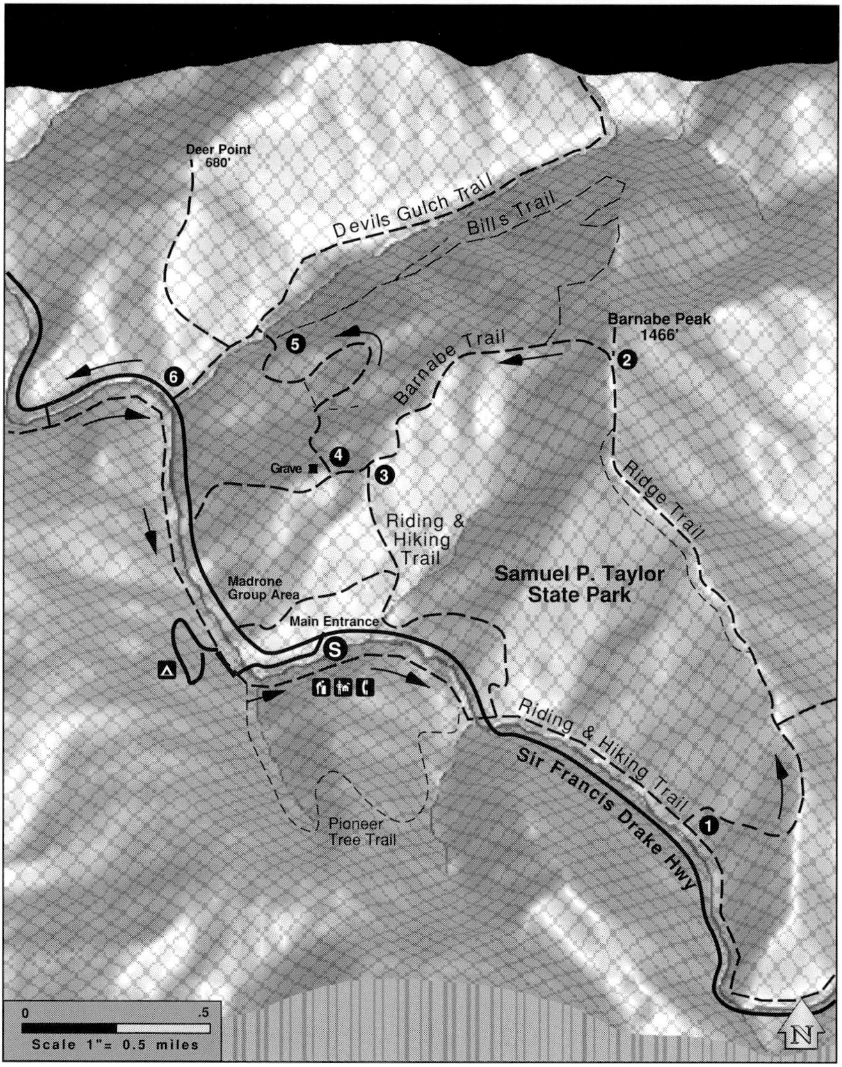

29 Bolinas Ridge Loop

Distance: 13.2 miles *Riding Time:* 1.5-2 hours
Elevation Change: 1300' *Difficulty:* Moderate
Technical Rating: 6 Steep fire road ascent.
After a steep climb, the trail becomes a gentle to moderate descent along a broad ridge top offering a pastoral, tranquil setting with grazing cows. Good views of Olema Valley to Tomales Bay.

Option: For an easier ride, start at the Bolinas Ridge Trailhead on Sir Francis Drake and do an out and back ride on Bolinas Ridge.

0.0 Start at the main entrance to Samuel P. Taylor State Park. Ride in past kiosk on road, then bear left to cross the bridge. Turn left again and take the bike path south along the creek.

1.0 Junction. Take Sir Francis Drake Hwy right towards Fairfax.

1.8 Shafter Bridge and junction ❶. Head right past the gate, right of the creek. After the first heavy winter rains, look for king salmon that swim up the creek from the ocean to spawn. Spawning salmon are usually three years old and undergo major changes as they end their lifecycle. Males turn brick red and their upper jaws distort forming a hook-like shape. Females often turn a dull bronze.

The ride leaves the canyon for a steep climb on the Riding & Hiking trail. There are a few deadend fire roads that come in from the left, one coming up from Kent Dam. Stay right and keep climbing.

3.4 Junction ❷ at 1300' with the Bolinas Ridge trail. Head right to begin a long gradual descent down Bolinas Ridge. As you head down the ridge, great views of the San Andreas Fault Zone open up to the west. It's hard to imagine that the opposite ridge (on Point Reyes) is slipping North at an average rate of 1.3" per year. Unfortunately, the motion comes in big spurts, the last one, 16' in 1906. The ride goes through a series of gates that keep the cows in, please close each one as you pass through it.

7.5 Junction with the Jewell trail. Stay left on Bolinas Ridge.

8.8 Junction ❸ with Sir Francis Drake. Head right downhill, then pick up the bike path (**9.5** mi.) that uses the old railroad bed. The North Pacific Coast Railroad began passenger service here in 1875. By the 1890s, up to 3000 people took the train to Camp Taylor on weekends to picnic, swim, camp and hike.

13.2 Main picnic area and park entrance.

Getting There

From Hwy 101:

In Greenbrae, W on Sir Francis Drake for 15.6 miles to the main entrance to Samuel P. Taylor State Park. Entrance fee.

Central Marin

Samuel P. Taylor State Park
Main Entrance

Elevation Profile

2000'
1500'
1000'
500'
Grade 24%
1
2
3
4
8
12
16

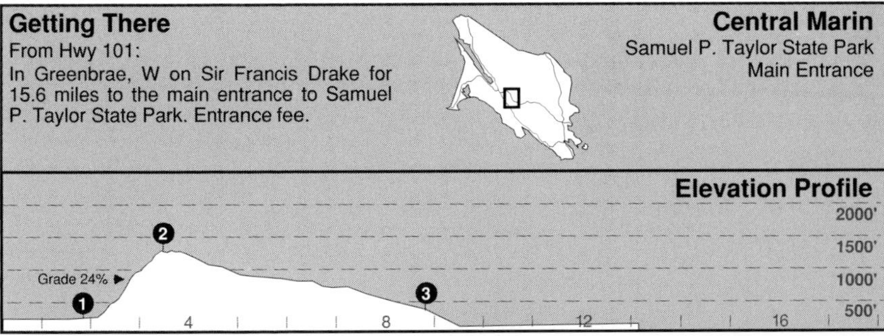

Sir Francis
Drake Hwy
Jewell Tr
Devils Gulch Trail
Barnabe Peak
1466'
Ridge Trail
Samuel P. Taylor
State Park
S
Bolinas Ridge
Bolinas Ridge Trail
1
2
3
1
Five
Brooks
0
.8
Scale 1" = 0.8 miles
N

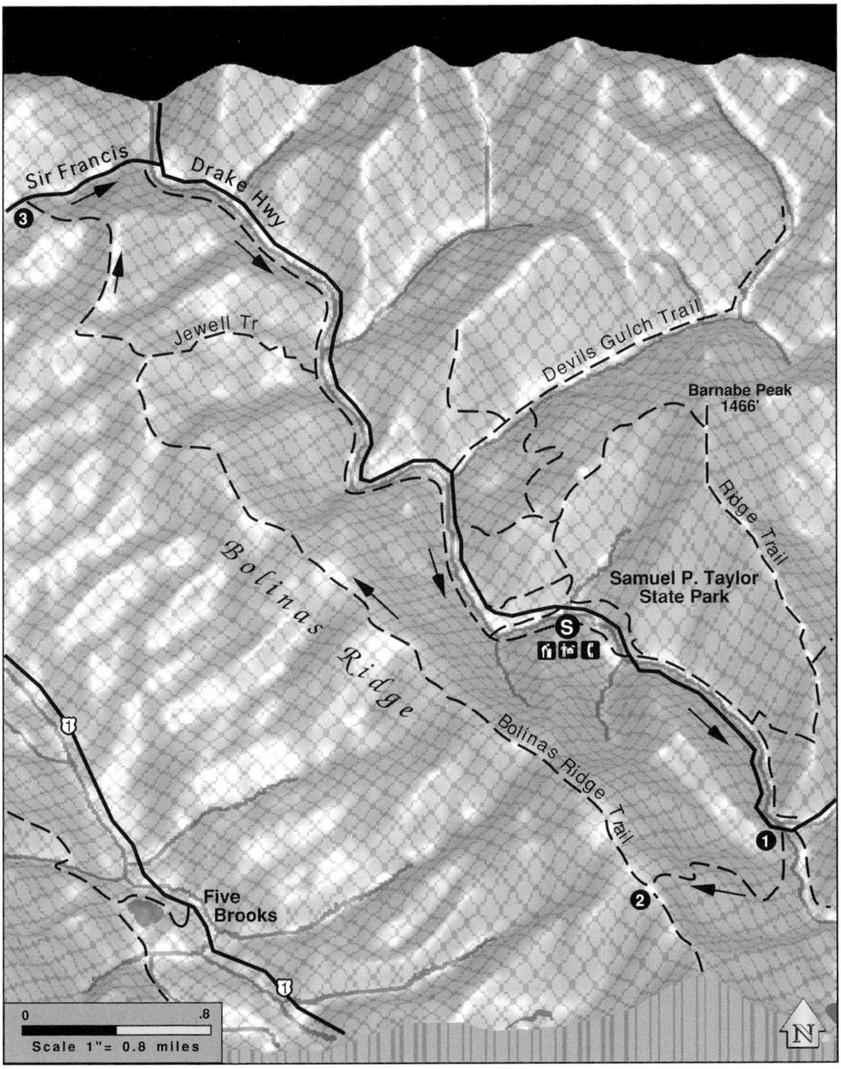

30 Las Gallinas Ponds - McInnis Park

Distance: 7.7 miles ***Riding Time:*** 1 hour
Elevation Change: 30' ***Difficulty:*** Easy
Technical Rating: 2 Flat levees with some ruts.

This is a flat ride on levees around the Las Gallinas Wildlife Ponds and McInnis Park on the bay, an ideal ride for beginners. It also is the best birding ride in Marin. Can be muddy in winter, thistles in summer.

0.0 From McInnis Park, continue north along Smith Ranch Rd. towards the Wildlife Ponds.

0.7 Junction ❶ and gate. Go left across the bridge, then left again on the signed "public path" to circle the inner pond clockwise. This 20 acre freshwater marsh holds treated water on its way to the bay. The small islands have been created to shelter birds. Look for ducks, geese and pelicans that enjoy the ponds so much that some have become permanent residents. All of the holding ponds are required during summer months when treated water can not be dumped into the bay.

1.4 Junction ❷. Head left on the main levee. Up ahead are salt water marshes that provide another variety of habitat. One rare and endangered bird you might see (or hear) is the California clapper rail, a drab-brown, hen-like bird that is found in salt marshes. During twilight, in the spring mating season, you can listen for pairs of birds exchanging a rapid clattering call.

2.2 Road change. The gravel road changes to dirt, which has some ruts. In winter, it can be very muddy; in summer, overgrown.

3.3 Junction ❸ and turnaround point. You can see the old runway and hangers of Hamilton Air Force Base across the canal and fields. The Air Force part of the base was closed in the 1970s. Currently, the Coast Guard operates helicopters here. Long-range plans call for the path to continue on through the base and around the bay.

5.9 Junction ❶ again. Head left through the sewage treatment plant. Just past the fence, go around the gate and take the levee road out towards the bay.

Note: In summer and fall, tall grasses may crowd the trail. If you ride over them, the grasses can wind around the rear hub and become difficult to remove. If that's the case, cut the ride short and head back the way you came. Otherwise, follow the levee around the marsh, all the way back to the parking area.

7.7 Parking area at McInnis Park.

Getting There

From Hwy 101:

In Terra Linda, R on Smith Ranch Rd to McInnis Park. Just after railroad tracks, L on Smith Ranch Rd. Park anywhere.

North Marin

McInnis Park
Main Playing Fields

Elevation Profile

2000'
1500'
1000'
500'
4 Flat Levees 8 12 16

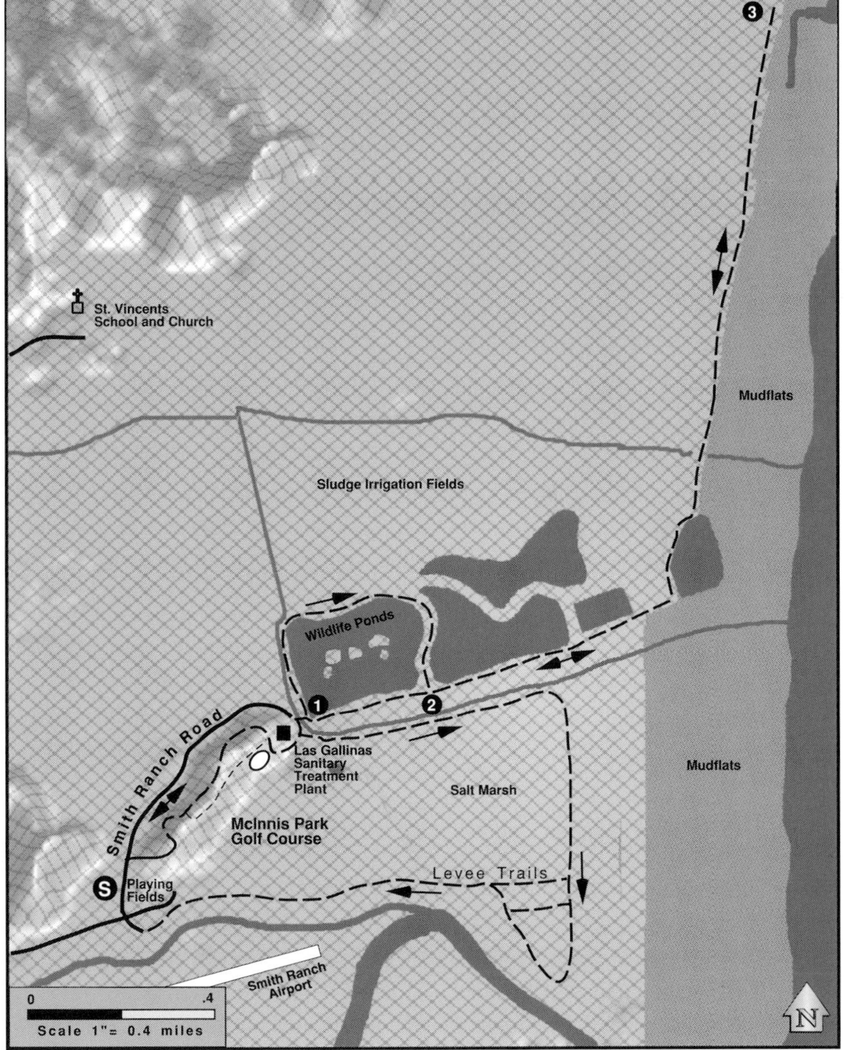

31 Terra Linda Ridge Loop

Distance: 8.7 miles *Riding Time:* 1.5-2 hours
Elevation Change: 1300" *Difficulty:* Moderate
Technical Rating: 6 Moderately steep climbs and descents.
A good after-work ride for locals, or a way to explore new neighborhoods with ridgetop views of surrounding hills. Multiple starting locations possible. Note: Cemetery gate hours 8am-5pm daily.

0.0 From the end of 5th Ave, ride through the cemetery gate 10', then go right along the fence to pick up a paved FR on a public access easement. Head uphill, then go right on the dirt road.

0.8 Water tank and junction ❶. Head left on either road and follow the ridge on a broad sometimes dusty FR. Some FR's and single tracks leave from this road to explore nearby hills.

1.6 Junction ❷. Go right and in 0.2 mi. ride out onto paved Fawn Drive. Take Fawn Dr. down the hill.

2.5 Junction with bike path. Go through the gate on the right and take the paved biking and hiking trail up to the saddle.

2.6 Junction ❸ at the saddle. Veer left to climb up onto Fox Lane trail, another FR that follows the ridge. Good views in all directions.

3.0 Junction. Go left (right is OK too, the two roads form a loop). The road dips and climbs over Sleepy Hollow below. At **3.5** miles, the road rejoins the other loop road.

3.7 Y-junction ❹. Go right to follow Terra Linda Ridge FR. You'll drop pretty steeply onto another ridgeline. **Note**: The FR left heads uphill 0.7 miles, then hits private property (George Lucas). It is expected that this trail will become accessible in the near future. If it happens, this ride will be extended to loop into Lucas Valley (no relation).

4.1 Junction. Stay straight (right) to traverse down the hill into Terra Linda. At **4.4** miles, the FR empties out onto paved Del Ganado Rd. Follow Del Ganado out to Manuel T. Freitas Parkway.

5.4 Freitas Parkway. Go right to ride up parkway in a series of rises.

6.1 Go through gate onto paved bike path and climb back up to the saddle where you end the loop section of this ride.

6.2 Junction ❸. Go straight on the bike path then left again on Fawn Drive, which heads back up to the ridge.

7.1 Junction ❷. Go left on the fairly level ridge heading back to the water tank, then go right down to the cemetery and car at **8.7** miles.

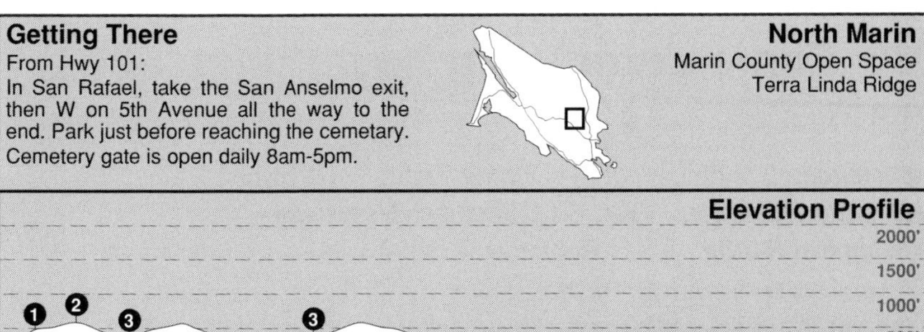

Getting There

From Hwy 101:
In San Rafael, take the San Anselmo exit, then W on 5th Avenue all the way to the end. Park just before reaching the cemetary. Cemetery gate is open daily 8am-5pm.

North Marin

Marin County Open Space
Terra Linda Ridge

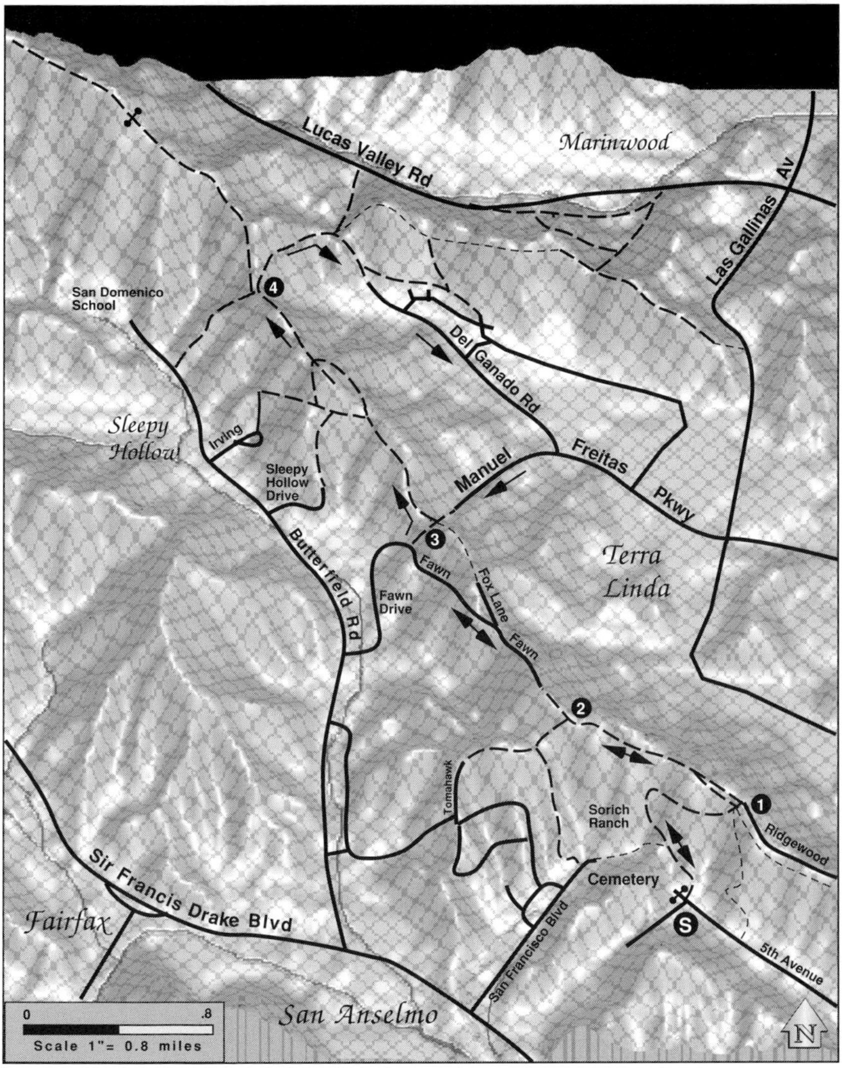

32 Loma Verde - Big Rock Ridge Loop

Distance: 11.7 miles ***Riding Time:*** 1.5-2 hours
Elevation Change: 1900' ***Difficulty:*** Strenuous
Technical Rating: 8 Some rocky climbing, very steep descent.

A tough hill climb ride for the strong minded. The ride takes you up rugged Big Rock Ridge, the second tallest mountain in Marin providing good views in all directions. Be prepared for a challenge!

0.0 Ride past the gate just south of Clay Ct. and up a steep private road to the tennis courts. To the right of the parking area is the Chicken Shack FR. Start up the FR that goes up and down on it's way up the ridge. The climbs range from gentle to brutal, but they are interspersed with flat or downhill respite. There are occasional parallel side trails off the main FR.

0.9 Junctions. Trails and roads enter from the right over the next 100 yds. Continue on the main FR.

2.3 Viewpoint. A clearing offers good views north to Mt. Burdell. At **2.7** mi. stay right past the Ponte FR.

3.4 Junction ❶ with Queenstone FR and Big Rock Ridge FR. Go right onto Big Rock Ridge FR.

Mt. Tam as seen from Big Rock Ridge

4.2 Junction ❷ with Luiz FR. (1493'). Continue up the Big Rock Ridge FR to a gate and private property at **4.5** mi. Big Rock (peak) lies one mile beyond at 1887', the 2nd tallest mountain in Marin. The tallest is Mt. Tamalpais, once known as the "sleeping lady" because of her profile, as seen in the photo (head at the left). At this point, turn around and head back down staying on Big Rock Ridge FR.

4.8 Junction ❷ again. Go right down Luiz FR. The road falls sharply down a south-facing ridge into Lucas Valley. The drop is fast and treacherous requiring good braking skills.

6.5 Junction ❸ with Creekside Drive. Go left and scout for a small paved bike trail 20 yds. on the right. At **6.8** miles, go left on Bridgegate Dr. to ride up into the Bridgegate neighborhood.

7.1 Connector path to Idylberry. Go right over to Idylberry Drive and follow it all the way back to Miller Creek (**9.9** mi.).Then go left.

10.6 Take the bike path along the freeway to Clay Ct. at **11.7** miles.

Getting There

From Hwy 101:

In Novato going north, take Nave Drive exit. Going south, take Alameda del Prado exit. Park on or near Clay Ct. on the west side of the Hwy 101 overpass.

North Marin

Marin County Open Space
Loma Verde

Elevation Profile

2000'
1500'
1000'
500'
Grade 24%
4
8
12
16

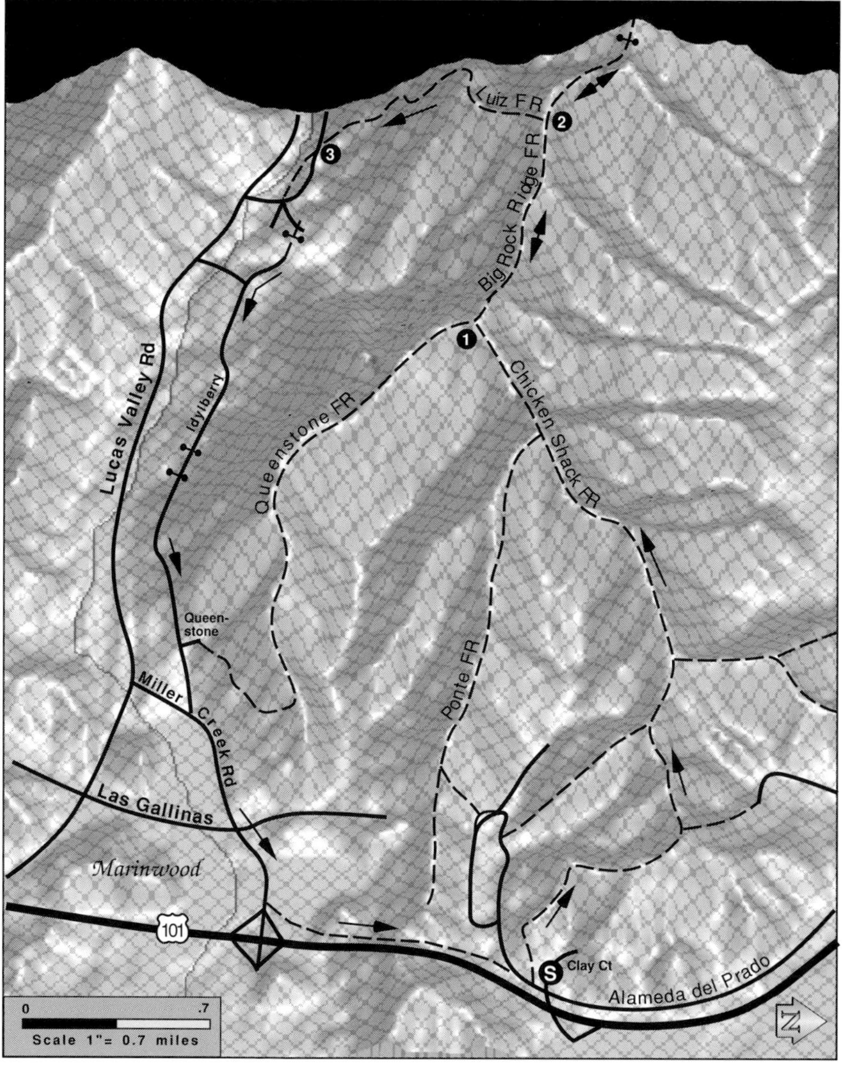

33 Mt. Burdell Loop

Distance: 8.3 miles ***Riding Time:*** 1.5-2 hours
Elevation Change: 1300' ***Difficulty:*** Moderate
Technical Rating: 7 Rocky climbing. Steep rocky descent.

Mt. Burdell presides over Novato's suburban valleys and pastoral slopes. A ride to it's peak is a rewarding trek. Some fire roads are rocky, some dusty or muddy. Good spring grasses and flowers.

0.0 Start at San Andreas Drive. Ride through the gate and up the FR. Up ahead, continue past a FR at **0.6** miles on the left.

0.8 Y-junction ❶. Go left onto Deer Camp FR. In the spring, this hillside provides magnificent, undulating green slopes. Mt. Burdell is to north Marin what Mt. Tam is to the south, a priceless treasure to be explored and cherished.

2.3 Junction ❷ with Cobblestone FR. Head left up the hill for the final short ascent to the top over, well-named, rocky terrain.

2.9 Junction ❸ with Burdell Mtn. Ridge Rd. (1450'). Go right to meander along the ridge and explore lookout spots. The road passes a quarry on the left, where cobblestones were mined by Chinese workers to line the streets of San Francisco in the 1870s. Remains of the mining process were dumped over the hill on the right. Ahead at **3.7** miles, the road ends at a private property gate (Buck Center for Aging). Turn around and head back to the Cobblestone junction.

4.3 Junction ❸ with Cobblestone FR. Go left down the FR. At **4.9** miles, continue past the Deer Camp FR to the Hidden Lake junction (**5.3** mi.). Go left on Middle Burdell FR. At **5.9** miles, you'll pass the junction of San Carlos FR. Stay on Middle Burdell FR. The road wanders through cattle gates and into oak-bay woodland. Mt. Burdell has the finest example of oak savannah and oak woodlands in Marin with five of California's nine species of oaks found here, including the valley, coast live, black, blue and Garry oak.

6.2 Y-junction ❷. Veer right to ride down along Salt Lick FR heading back towards the start. Pass San Marin FR on the left at **6.6** miles.

6.8 Junction of San Carlos FR. Ride left down to the San Marin FR that forms a fire break for the community just beyond.

7.3 Junction ❸ with San Marin FR. Go right to travel along the perimeter of the open space. There's a short steep hill before the road joins another road coming from the right. Continue left along the FR to the gate where you started at **8.3** miles.

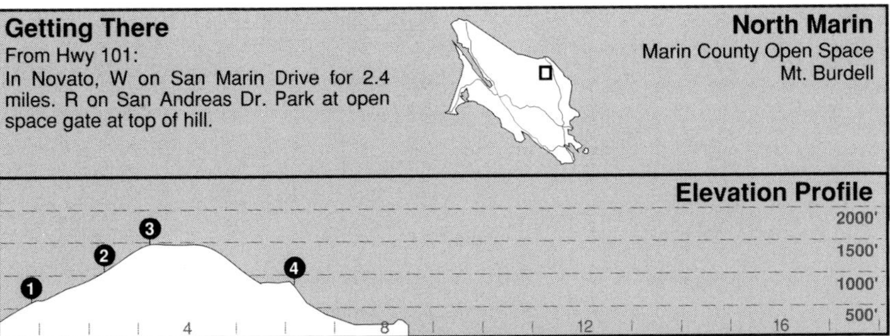

Burdell Mtn Ridge Rd
Private
Mt Burdell
1558'
Olompali State Historic Park
Cobblestone FR
Deer Camp FR
Private
Private
Old Quarry Trail
Middle
Burdell FR
Hidden Lake
890'
Buck Center for Aging
Private
San Andreas FR
San Carlos FR
Salt Lick FR
Fieldstone Tr
Big Tank FR
Michako Tr
San Marin FR
San Marin FR
San Andreas Drive
Simmons Ln
Butterfield Dr
Wood Hollow
San Marin Drive
Novato
0
.5
Scale 1" = 0.5 miles
N

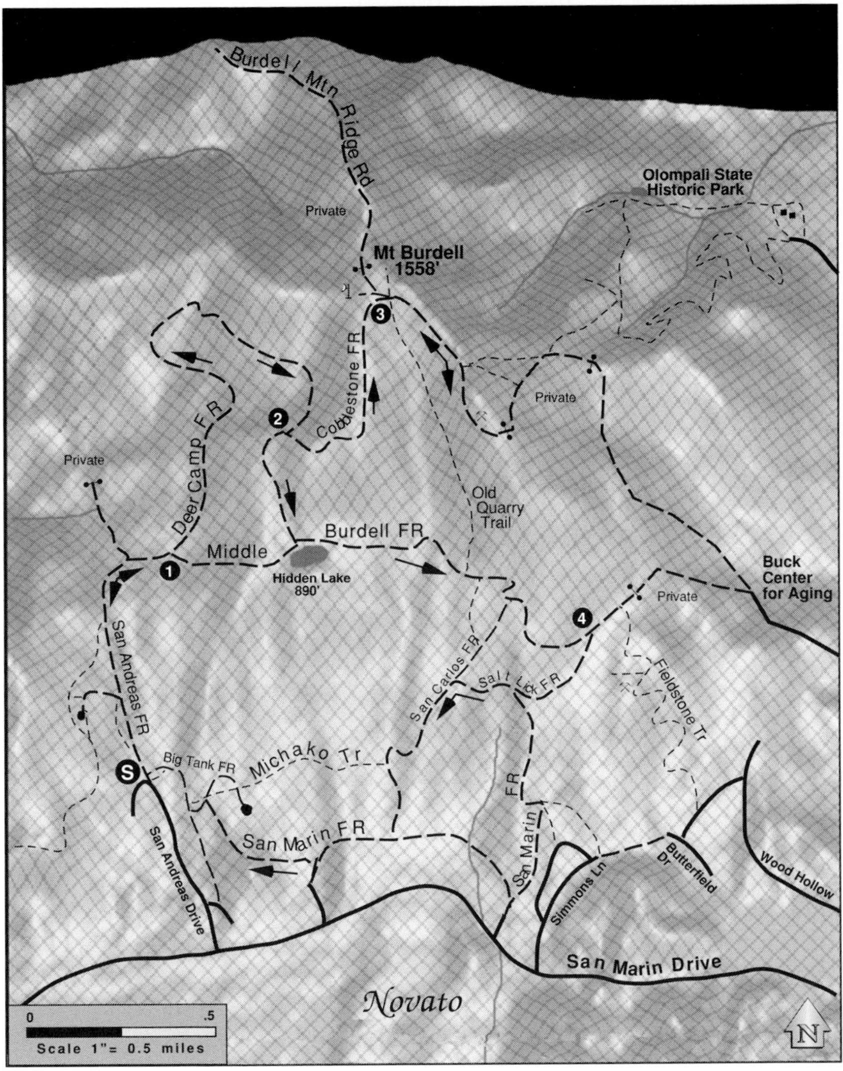

34 Rush Creek

Distance: 4.6 miles ***Riding Time:*** 1 hour
Elevation Change: 100' ***Difficulty:*** Easy
Technical Rating: 2 All fire road.

This easy ride skirts a tidal marsh offering shorebird viewing in the fall and wildflower viewing in the spring. A fairly level road with only a few small bumps and ruts make this ideal for beginners. Can be windy.

Note: Views of the marsh are best at high tide, which occurs about 2 hours later than those shown in tide table for the Golden Gate Bridge.

0.0 From the road, head through the open space gate on the fire road. Tall reeds along the marsh provide cover and allow you to ease up closer to fall and winter shorebirds, egrets, pelicans and ducks.

Mt. Burdell

Mt. Burdell looms up across the freeway. In the center of the mountain, you can see the controversial Buck Center for the Aging. The building lies on land called "unstable" by a geologist in the 1970s, advice that was forgotten by the 1990s. To the left of the building on the flat area, there used to be a large earthen berm, built by the Buck Center, that was later removed. The berm was felt to be partly responsible for earth movement and house buckling in the Partridge Knolls subdivision down to the left.

1.0 Rush Creek. Rush Creek is more distinguishable from the marsh as it passes close to the road here.

1.2 Junction ❶. In the middle of a small grove of bay and oak trees, a single track leads down and across a low-lying levee, cutting off a small inlet. Continue on the FR, which is overgrown and becomes more like a single track.

1.7 Junction ❷ and drainage creek. In the winter and spring during heavy runoff, this crossing may be difficult. New houses built in 1998 and a cemetery lie inland.

2.3 Junction ❸ and turn-around point. This is the end of open space. Hopefully, some day the land beyond will become open space, and the road, which continues for another 1.7 miles, will be rideable.

Getting There

From Hwy 101:
In Novato, take Atherton offramp heading east, immediate L on Binford Rd. Go 200 yds. and park near open space gate.

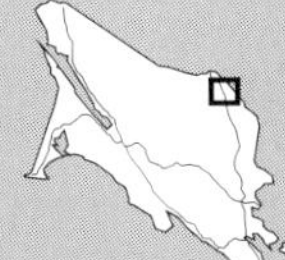

North Marin

Marin County Open Space
Rush Creek

Elevation Profile

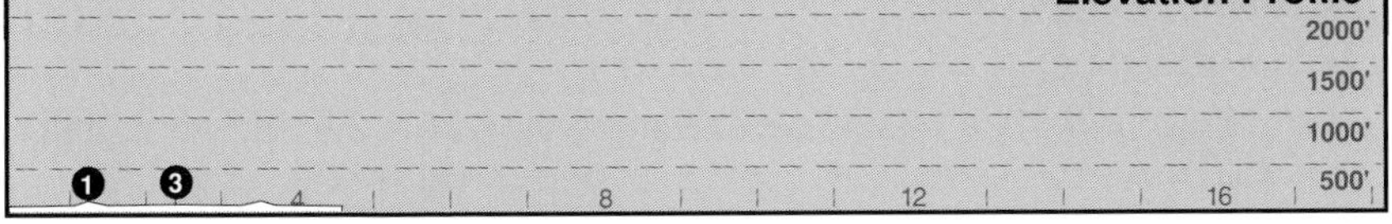

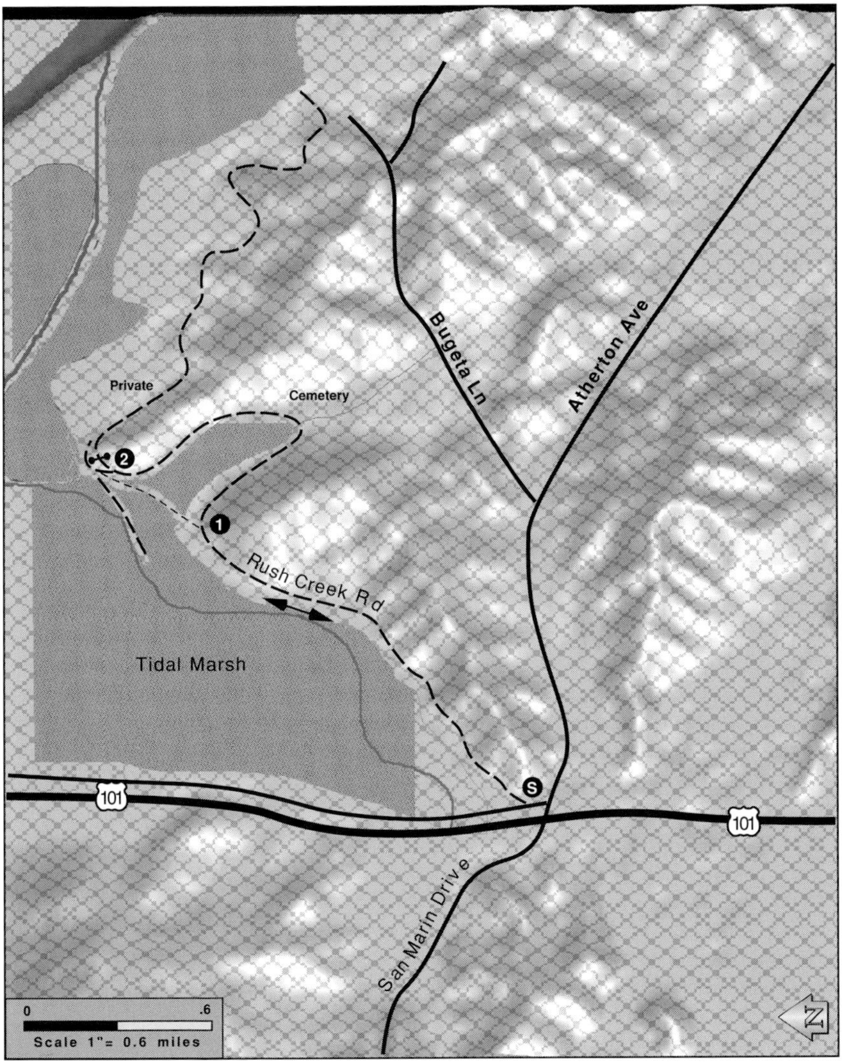

2000'
1500'
1000'
500'
1
3
4
8
12
16

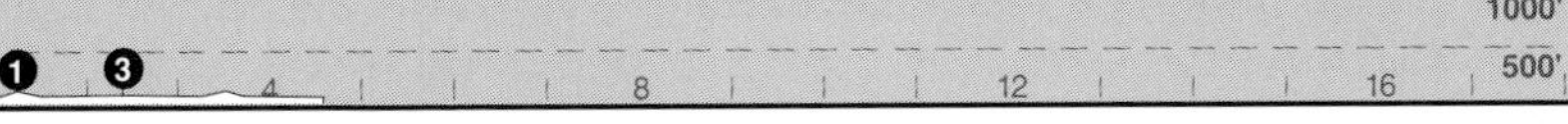

Private
Cemetery
Bugeta Ln
Atherton Ave
2
1
Rush Creek Rd
Tidal Marsh
S
101
101
San Marin Drive
0
.6
Scale 1"= 0.6 miles
N

35 Bear Valley Trail

Distance: 6.2 miles *Riding Time:* 1 hour
Elevation Change: 400' *Difficulty:* Easy
Technical Rating: 2 Smooth fire road all the way.
This out and back ride makes a great family ride on the most popular trail at Point Reyes. The ride makes a gentle climb along a beautiful creek setting to Divide Meadow, then drops towards the coast.

Note: Bring a bike lock so you can lock your bike and hike the last mile out to a spectacular coastline at Arch Rock and Drakes Bay.

0.0 Start at the Bear Valley trailhead at the south end of the parking area and head into the meadow. Look for deer along the way. If you see some unusual-looking deer, white or black, they are the non-native fallow deer introduced in the 1940s.

Bear Valley Visitor Center

0.5 Floods and alders. People still talk about the storm of 1982. Bear Valley was completely blocked by flood debris and over one-half of the trail was destroyed. One of the few remaining signs of the flood are groves of young red alders that seeded the following spring. In time, these alders will get much larger, once again shading the trail.

1.6 Junction ❶ at Divide Meadow. In the early 1890s, the Pacific Union Club of San Francisco built a sportsman's lodge here with 35 rooms, stables and kennels. The original plans included a golf course, tennis courts and swimming pool. Fortunately, the entire resort was never built. The lodge building deteriorated and was removed in 1950. You might be able to discover its location on the east side of the meadow hilltop. The ride continues with an easy descent.

3.1 Junction ❷ with the Glen and Baldy trails. Bicycles must stop here. When ready, ride back to the Visitor Center at **6.2** miles.

Option: Hike one mile to the Arch Rock overlook with great views of the coast. About 50' from the overlook, a short, well-used trail drops steeply down to Coast Creek and out to the beach and ocean. It is worth the trip down to glimpse the sea tunnel (the "arch" of Arch Rock) where the creek meets the ocean.

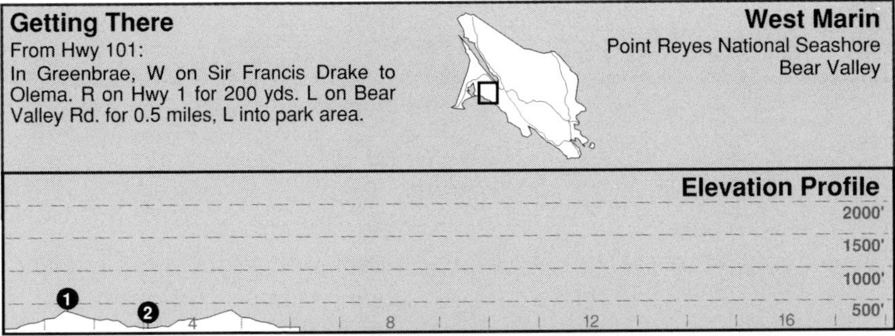

Getting There

From Hwy 101:

In Greenbrae, W on Sir Francis Drake to Olema. R on Hwy 1 for 200 yds. L on Bear Valley Rd. for 0.5 miles, L into park area.

West Marin

Point Reyes National Seashore

Bear Valley

Elevation Profile

2000'
1500'
1000'
500'
1
2
4
8
12
16

Bear Valley Rd
1
Sir Francis Drake
Sky Camp
Bear Valley
S
Sky Trail
Olema
Meadow Trail
Bear Valley Trail
Sky Trail
Old Pine Trail
1
1
Sky Trail
Coast Trail
Baldy Trail
2
Bear Valley Trail
Glen Camp
Arch Rock
0
.9
Scale 1"= 0.9 miles
N

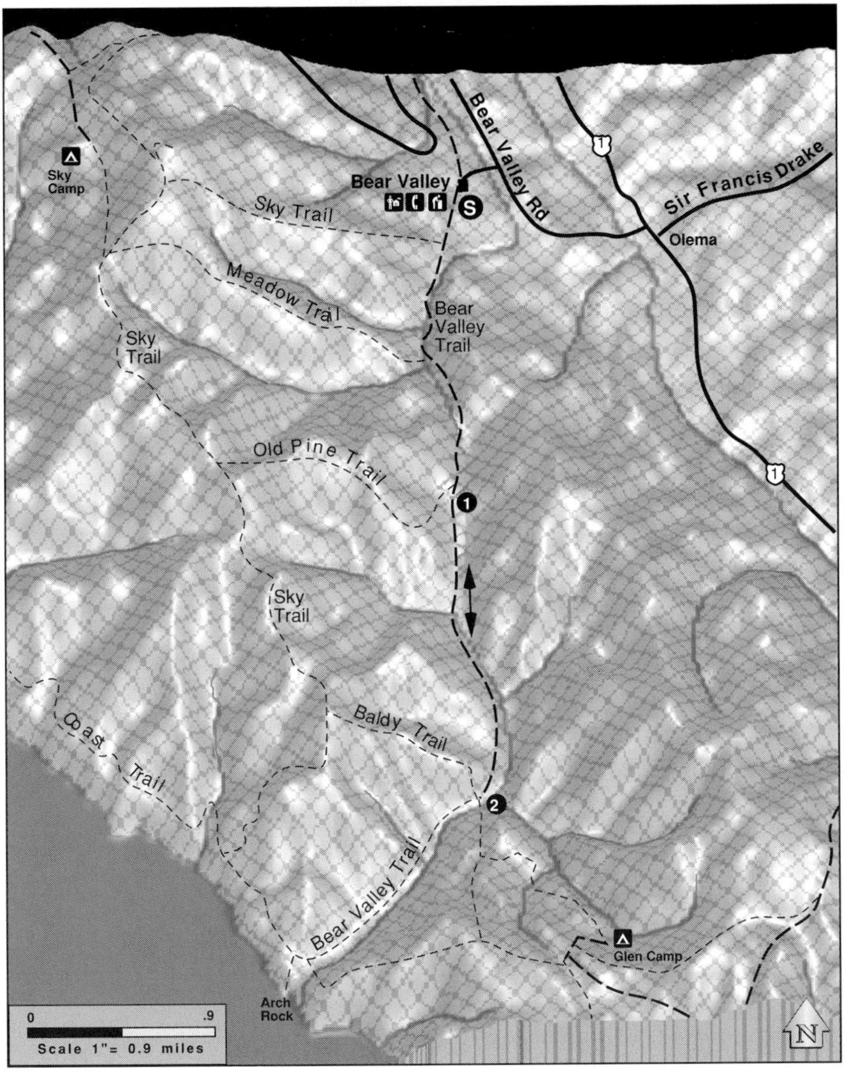

36 Five Brooks to Wildcat Camp

Distance: 13.0 miles *Riding Time:* 2 hours
Elevation Change: 2300' *Difficulty:* Moderate to strenuous
Technical Rating: 7 Some steep climbs and descents.
An out and back ride that takes you over Inverness Ridge to the wild coastline of Point Reyes. It's a heart-pumping climb on the way back, so bring your climbing legs. Can be foggy on the ridge and coast.

0.0 From the Five Brooks Trailhead, ride out the paved road to a junction at **0.2** miles. Go right to start up the wide, easy Stewart FR. The road climbs in a steady manner up towards a peak known as Fir Top. This side of the hill is north-facing, so you have lots of shade as you climb through the woods of bays, oaks and Douglas firs.

3.0 Junction ❶. Stay right to continue on Stewart trail, which was once a two-lane paved road used for logging in the 1950s.

3.8 Crest of the hill at Fir Top (1320'). The trees have a sweet smell up here. It is often cool and moist on Inverness Ridge, from fog that is almost a daily occurrence in the summertime. The trail now drops sharply towards the coast with an occasional short rise.

5.2 Junction ❷ with Glen trail. Stay left to continue down the hill. As you round some of the corners, glimpses of the ocean peek out, enticing you down towards the beach. The terrain is ruggedly beautiful out here, and the road gets brake-wrenchingly steep as you drop into the small valley where Wildcact Camp is located. On one of our rides, we surprised a grey fox here as it was crossing the road.

6.5 Wildcat Camp. This is one of the four backpacking camps on Point Reyes. All are accessible by bike if you are looking for a camping adventure. Be sure to head down to the beach to take in the ocean and a view (or hike) to Alamere Falls, about a mile south. In the spring, this is one of the most scenic waterfalls in Marin, a 50' cascade onto the beach. After your break and some nourishment, return the way you came. The worst of the climb is in the beginning mile or so, so take heart and keep on pedaling.

7.8 Junction ❷. If you'd like more exercise, go left to visit Glen Camp, the most secluded of all the camps as it sits in a small pocket valley, surrounded by trees. Otherwise, go right for a steady climb.

8.2 Fir Top. Crest the hill and enjoy the fast cruise down the FR.

12.8 Junction. Turn left to zip back to the trailhead at **13.0** miles.

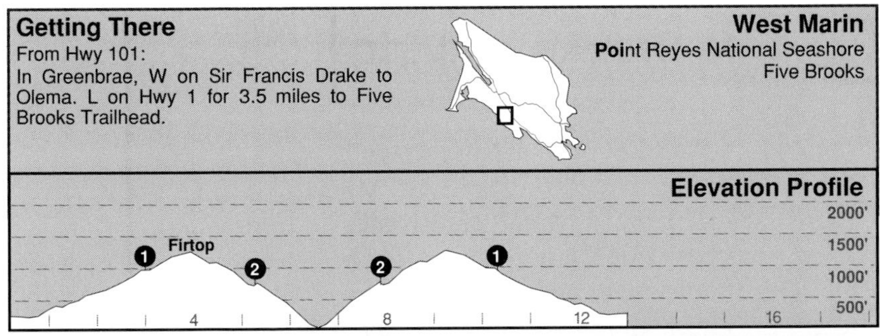

Getting There

From Hwy 101:

In Greenbrae, W on Sir Francis Drake to Olema. L on Hwy 1 for 3.5 miles to Five Brooks Trailhead.

West Marin

Point Reyes National Seashore

Five Brooks

Elevation Profile

2000'
1500'
1000'
500'
Firtop
1
2
2
1
4
8
12
16

Greenpicker Trail
Bear Valley Trail
1
Five Brooks
S
Stewart Trail
Firtop 1324'
Olema Valley Tr
Greenpicker Trail
Glen Camp
1
Ridge Trail
Glen Trail
2
Coast Trail
Stewart Trail
Alamere Creek
Mud Lake
Coast Trail
Wildcat Camp
Wildcat Lake
0
.7
Scale 1"= 0.7 miles
N

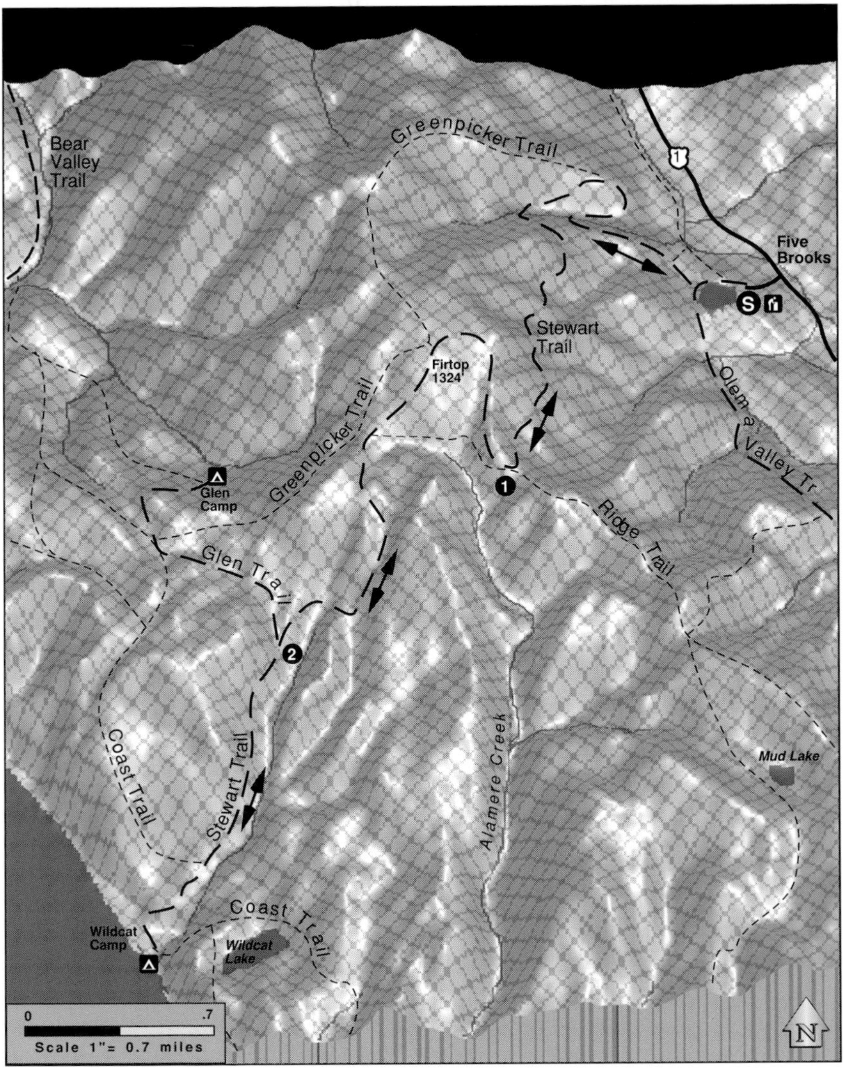

37 Five Brooks - Bolinas Ridge Loop

Distance: 21.4 miles ***Riding Time:*** 2.5-3 hours
Elevation Change: 3000' ***Difficulty:*** Strenuous
Technical Rating: 6 Some downhill speed control required.
A big adventure that takes you from the gorgeous Olema Valley to the ridge top above it. Long ride with lots of climbing, but totally worth the effort. Grand views of Bolinas Lagoon.

0.0 Start at Five Brooks Trailhead and head out the FR. Take the left at the signs onto a single track to go counter-clockwise around the overgrown pond area.

0.2 Junction with Olema Valley trail. Go left on Olema trail. The trail starts out by climbing through trees to a saddle at 800' where it intersects with Bolema trail at **1.4** miles. Stay on Olema Valley trail and cruise down a less traveled single track that breaks out into open grassland and shrubs and continues down the valley.

2.7 Junction ❶ with Randall Spur trail. Continue straight. If shrubs crowd the trail, watch out for stinging nettles and poison oak. Up ahead, you come back into shaded creek drainages, where you must ford one creek and cross another on a bridge.

5.7 Junction ❷. Ride south on Hwy 1.

6.9 Junction ❸ of Bolinas-Fairfax Rd. This junction is unsigned but it is opposite the road to Bolinas. Go left across the highway and cross the cattle guard onto the paved road up to the ridge. It's a long climb, so pace yourself. The grade is steady and not too steep, with beautiful views of Bolinas Lagoon visible at turnouts along the way.

11.2 Junction ❹ at the crest of Bolinas-Fairfax Rd. (1520'). Take the FR that is on your left. This is Bolinas Ridge FR and will climb and dip its way back along the ridge. Pass McCurdy FR at **14.7** miles. The ridge is mostly wooded in this section.

16.2 Junction ❺ with the Randall trail FR. Take a left around the gate to swoop back into Olema Valley. **Option**: Continue straight for 0.5 miles for some spectacular views down Bolinas Ridge, then return here. The FR winds around corners so speed control is important.

17.9 Junction of Hwy 1. Cross the highway and catch the Randall Spur single track to the Olema Valley trail and junction ❶. Go right on Olema Valley trail to gently climb to the saddle at Bolema trail at **20.0** mile. Then sharply drop down along the creek. Don't miss the last right turn to reach the Five Brooks Trailhead at **21.4** miles.

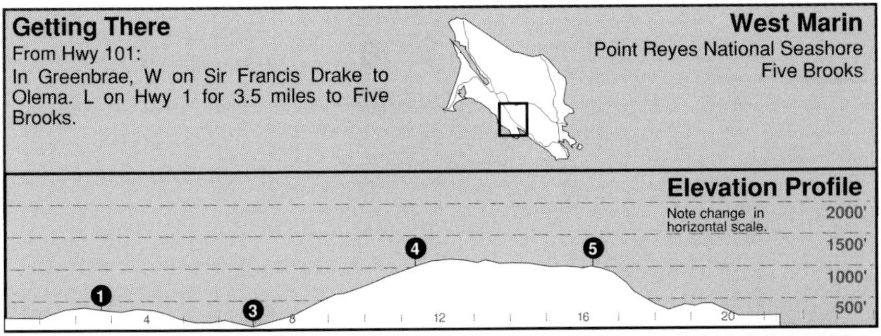
Getting There
From Hwy 101:
In Greenbrae, W on Sir Francis Drake to Olema. L on Hwy 1 for 3.5 miles to Five Brooks.
West Marin
Point Reyes National Seashore
Five Brooks
Elevation Profile
Note change in horizontal scale.
2000'
1500'
1000'
500'
4
8
12
16
20

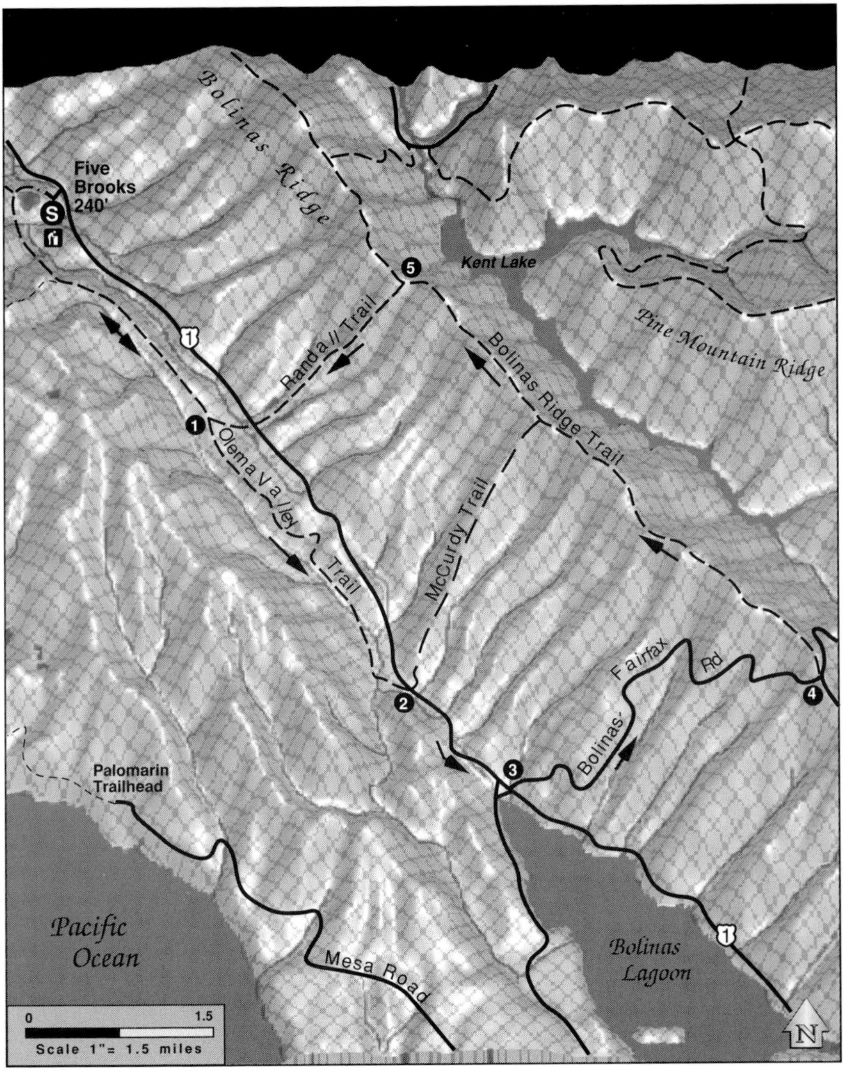

Bolinas Ridge
Five Brooks 240'
Kent Lake
Randall Trail
Bolinas Ridge Trail
Pine Mountain Ridge
Olema Valley Trail
McCurdy Trail
Fairfax Rd
Bolinas
Palomarin Trailhead
Pacific Ocean
Mesa Road
Bolinas Lagoon
0
1.5
Scale 1"= 1.5 miles
N

38 Inverness Ridge Loop

Distance: 11.1 miles ***Riding Time:*** 1.5-2 hours
Elevation Change: 1900' ***Difficulty:*** Moderate
Technical Rating: 7 Narrow single track and steep descent
This ride has a challenging single track trail in the renowned Point Reyes National Seashore. Highlights include the bishop pine forest recovering from a major fire and views of Tomales Bay.

0.0 Start at White House Pool parking area. From the lot, go right onto Sir Francis Drake Hwy, which immediately curves right.

0.1 Turn left onto Balboa Ave, which winds quickly up through a quaint neighborhood and then settles into a steady climb to the ridge. At an early Y-junction, stay left on Balboa.

1.6 Junction ❶ at top of Balboa. Ride around the gate at the end of the road onto Limantour Rd. and go right. This area is part of the 1995 wildfire that swept through 12,000 acres on Point Reyes. The regrowth is impressive here, small trees and seedlings abound.

2.1 Parking area and junction ❷. Take Inverness Ridge FR north towards Mt. Vision. This dual track skirts along the ridge and dumps out at **3.2** miles onto a driveway dominated by a large house on the ridgetop ahead. Go 200' up the driveway and catch the trail again on the left. This time however, the trail is a narrow overgrown single track that challenges your technical climbing skills. Notable is the remarkable regrowth of manzanita, a green, small-leaved shrub. The trail climbs up to a ridge, down into a saddle, then up again.

4.7 FAA Radar station/Pt. Reyes Hill. Paved road from here takes you along the ridge towards Mt.Vision, Point Reyes lays before you in all its glory. At **5.2** miles, you come out through a gate. Ride down the road another 0.8 mi. to a parking area on the right.

6.0 Gate and junction ❸. Take the FR down the hill, entering Tomales Bay State Park. The FR is steep in sections and winds around some hairpin turns. Go past a gate at about **6.9** miles and continue downhill. In another 0.1 mile you see a junction, turn left downhill.

7.2 Gate and paved road. Go down this road, Perth Way. At all the junctions ahead, continue downhill towards Tomales Bay. The roads change names here, so you end up taking Perth to Forres to Mesa to Edgemont to Laurel View to Hawthorne. Finally, take a left onto Inverness Way past a firehouse to Sir Francis Drake Hwy.

8.2 SF Drake. Go right on the highway back to the car (**11.1** miles).

Getting There

From Hwy 101:

In Greenbrae, W on Sir Francis Drake to Olema, R on Hwy 1 for 200 yds. L on Bear Valley Rd. R on Sir Francis Drake for 100 yds. L into White House Pool parking area.

West Marin

Point Reyes National Seashore
White House Pool

Elevation Profile

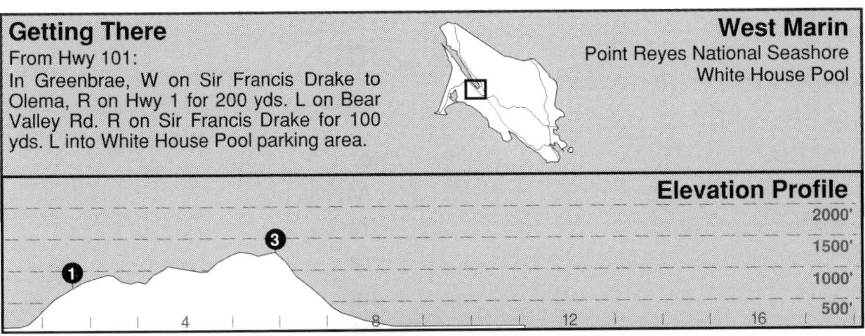

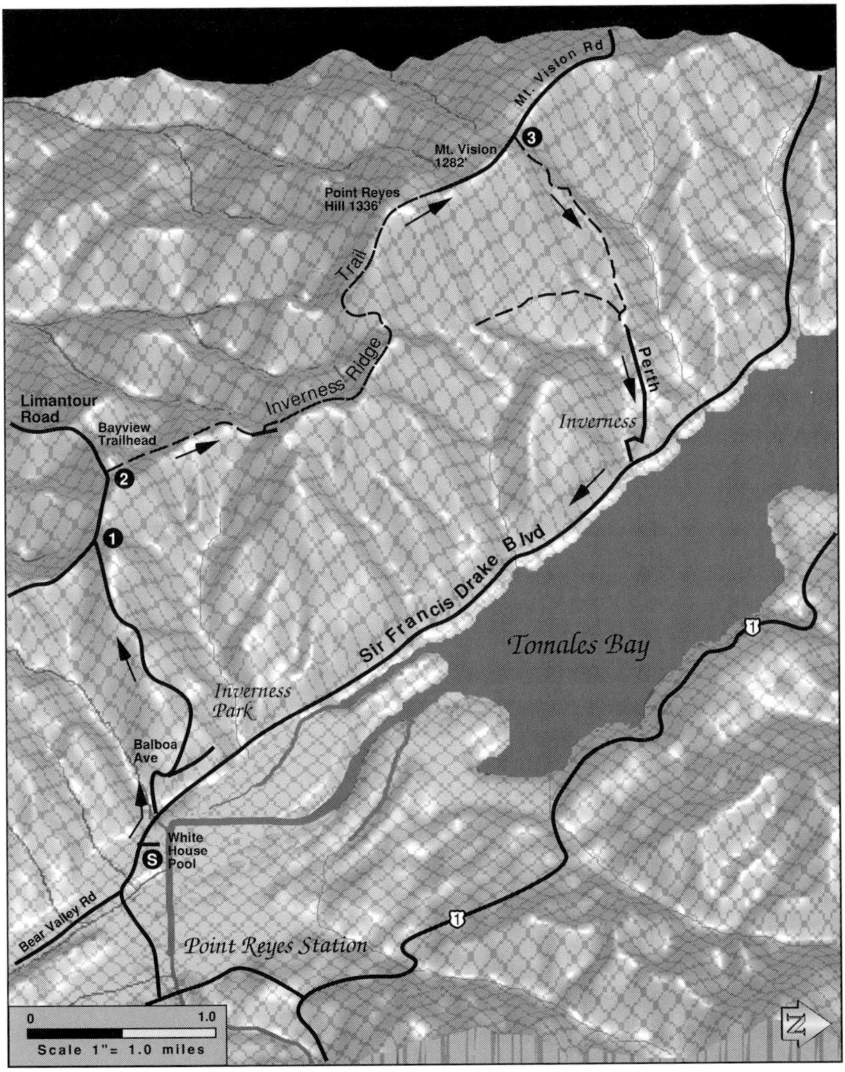

39 Estero Trail to Drakes Head

Distance: 9.2 miles ***Riding Time:*** 1.5-2 hours
Elevation Change: 1200' ***Difficulty:*** Moderate
Technical Rating: 7 Some single track that is rutted and pitted. On a clear day this destination ride is spectacular! Bring a lunch and plan a layover on the majestic bluffs of Drakes Head for the incredible views. The single track offers some challenges too.

Note: At the time we went to press, this trail was officially closed at the bridge at 1.1 mile due to slides from El Nino 1998. The park service is not sure if, or how, it will be reopened. To check the status of the trail or let them know you are interested in it, call the park at 415-663-1092. We have written this ride describing the old trail.

0.0 From the Estero Trailhead, take the Estero trail as it traipses across a hillside and through an old overgrown Christmas tree farm.

1.1 Levee across Home Bay. Ride across the levee and up along the bank. The trail takes you over a knoll overlooking Home Bay and Johnsons Oyster Farm, and down over another levee.

2.6 Signed junction ❶. Go left on the trail to Drakes Head, which becomes little more than a worn cow path over a grassy knoll. **Option**: Continue straight for a side trip to Sunset Beach, which lies about 1.5 miles away. Often, you can see harbor seals near there.

2.8 The trail hits a cow watering pond and some fences. Go across the people gate and veer left on a FR along a fenceline. Another trail marker sits along the fenceline.

3.0 Another person gate. Continue along the fenceline path.

3.2 Junction ❷ and cattle chute. A sign directs you to take a right turn after going through the people gate to get to Drakes Head. Ride out the bluff on the meandering, branching path. The trail seems clear in some areas and peters out in other areas. Stay on the more southern bluff heading towards the ocean. Down to your left at **4.2** miles, there is a water tank and trees, site of the Drakes Head Ranch that operated from the 1850s to 1960.

4.6 Drakes Head. The headland lies atop sheer cliffs. Stay back from the edge! Take a sojourn to check out the marvelous vista. Limantour Beach runs southeast to the left. Estero Lagoon meets the ocean to the south. To the southwest, we can see Chimney Rock and Pt. Reyes. From here retrace your steps back the way you came.

9.2 Back at the trailhead parking area.

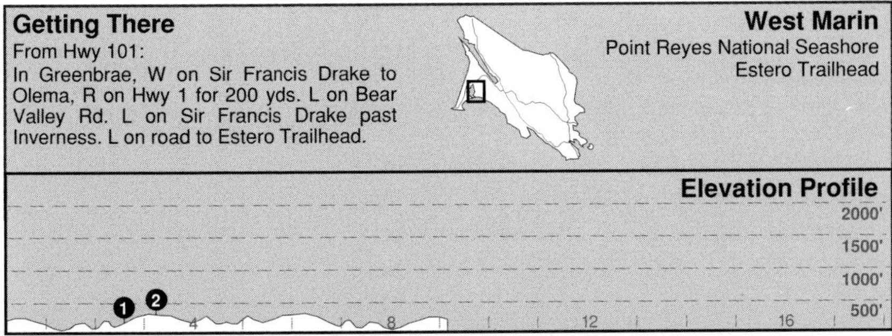
Getting There
From Hwy 101:
In Greenbrae, W on Sir Francis Drake to Olema, R on Hwy 1 for 200 yds. L on Bear Valley Rd. L on Sir Francis Drake past Inverness. L on road to Estero Trailhead.
West Marin
Point Reyes National Seashore
Estero Trailhead
Elevation Profile
2000'
1500'
1000'
500'
4
8
12
16

Sir Francis Drake Hwy
Oyster Farm
Schooner Bay
Estero Trail
Home Ranch
Home Bay
Drakes Estero
Sunset Beach Trail
Estero Trail
White Gate Trail
Estero Trail
Drakes Head Trail
Sunset Beach
Limantour Estero
Drakes Head
Limantour Spit
0
.9
Scale 1" = 0.9 miles
N

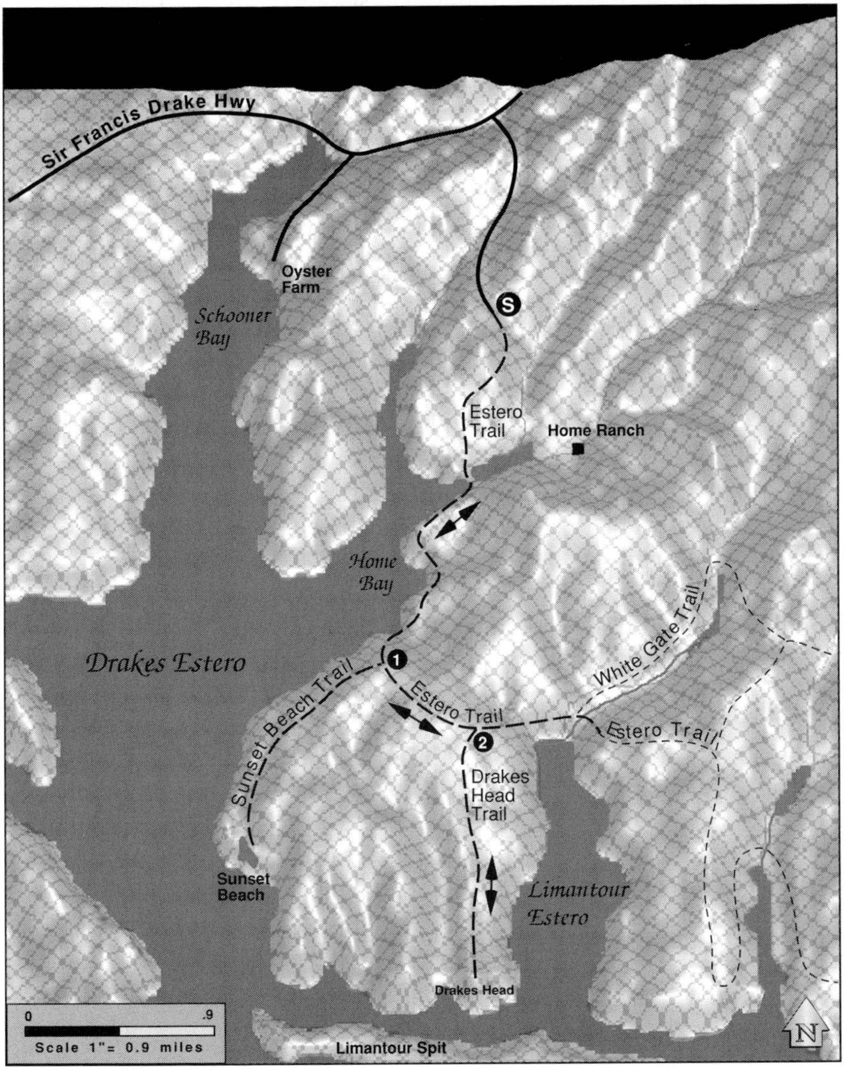

40 Marshall Beach and Abbotts Lagoon

Distance: 13.8 miles ***Riding Time:*** 2 hours
Elevation Change: 700' ***Difficulty:*** Moderate
Technical Rating: 3 Broad fire road, one steep ascent.
Over hill and dale you go in this ride through the wonderfully pristine and serene northern Point Reyes peninsula with views of Tomales Bay. Great wildflowers in spring. Can be very windy and/or foggy!

0.0 Start at the junction of Pierce Point Rd. and Marshall Beach Rd. There's a small turnout a couple of hundred yards up the road, just before the first cattle guard, where you can park. Ride over the cattle guard (keep up your speed and stay perpendicular to the bars) onto a wide FR that gently descends on a peninsula with views north.

1.0 L Ranch junction. Continue straight on main road.

1.4 Y-junction. Veer onto left FR. The road becomes a bit less wide here and you climb over a series of gentle rises to see the next vista.

2.5 Marshall Beach Trailhead and junction ❶. Go straight around the gate. The trail meanders through open grass fields with wonderful views of Tomales Bay before dropping sharply into the cove and the beach. Look for great wildflowers in March and April, especially the deep blue iris and the low-growing, bluish-white lily, called hairy cats ears; check the flower up close to see how it got its name.

3.8 Marshall Beach and junction ❷. This picturesque beach offers sunbathing, picnicking, wading and great views across Tomales Bay. If you head north along the beach, you might find traces of Miwok shell mounds. Or take the time for a quiet visit with nature before heading back. Return the way you came.

7.6 Parking area. To continue the ride, head out to the road and go right to make a winding descent along the Pierce Point Rd.

9.6 Abbotts Lagoon parking area and junction ❸. Take the trail left out towards the ocean. The bottom half of the trail may be rutted from damage due to El Nino in 1998.

10.7 Junction ❹. The bike trail ends here. There is good birding in the lagoon, with many ducks and other waterfowl in the fall and winter. In the spring, there are some great wildflowers on the hill towards the south. You can also lock your bike and hike across the bridge to the ocean another half-mile away. When done exploring, head back to the car at **13.8** miles. **Note**: You can drive to the end of Pierce Point Rd. for more views, and a chance to see Tule elk.

Getting There

From Hwy 101:

In Greenbrae, W on Sir Francis Drake to Olema. R on Hwy 1 for 200 yds. L on Bear Valley Rd. L on Sir Francis Drake, R on Pierce Point Rd. R on Marshall Beach Rd.

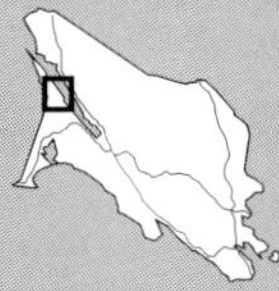

West Marin

Point Reyes National Seashore

Marshall Beach

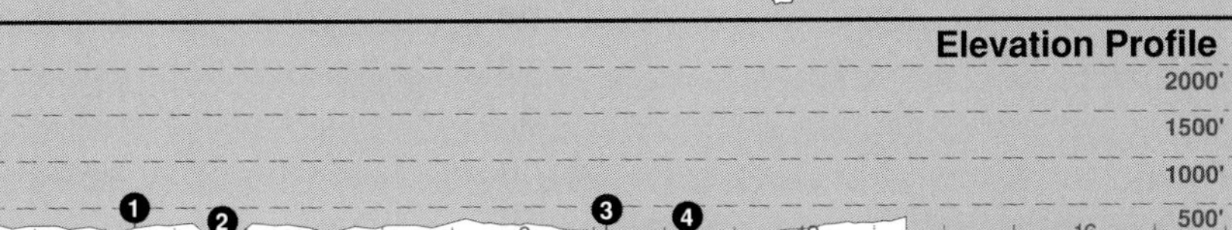

Elevation Profile

2000'
1500'
1000'
500'
1
2
3
4
4
8
12
16

1
Marshall Beach
2
Lairds Landing
Tomales Bay
Kehoe Beach
1
Pacific Ocean
Marshall Beach Rd
Tomales Bay State Park
S
3
Abbotts Lagoon
4
Pierce Point Rd
0
.8
Scale 1" = 0.8 miles
N

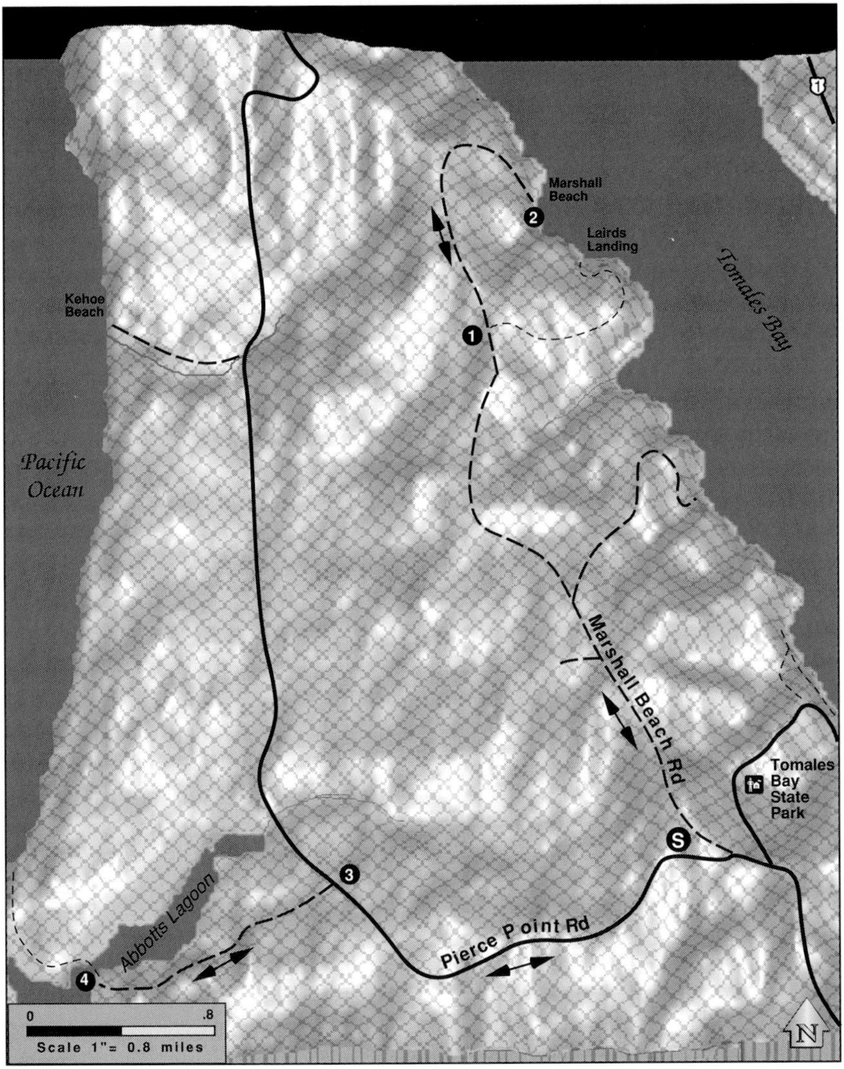

A1 Bike Maintenance and Repair

Mountain bikes are rugged, tough pieces of equipment. But like any piece of equipment, they need to be maintained. Keep your bike in good condition by inspecting it between rides, fixing loose, worn or broken parts, and keeping the drive-train clean and lubricated.

Pre-Ride Checklist

1. Check tire pressure. Set to correspond to your ride. Rocky trails require higher pressure and loose dirt lower pressure.
2. Check brake levers and pads to be sure both are working properly.
3. Check tires for cuts, punctures or worn sidewalls (may be caused by brake pads rubbing them).
4. Make sure chain and derailleurs are clean and well lubricated.
5. Bounce the bike and check for loose bolts, including pedals.
6. Check the headset by wriggling the handlebars while holding the brakes, if they're loose you'll feel some play. Check the bottom bracket by wiggling crank arms, if they're loose you'll feel some play.

What to Carry - Tools and Supplies

Some people carry only a minimal set of tools like patch kit and pump. However, we recommend a more complete kit that will get you by most common problems, yet is not too heavy. Groups can always share tools to reduce weight.

Spoke wrench: We carry the Black Park tool.

Chain tool: Examine a full-sized Park chain tool and find a travel-size chain tool with similar features.

Screwdriver: We use a very small, four-way (interchangeable) screwdriver from the hardware store.

Allen wrenches: Carry 4, 5, 6mm with 2 and 3mm optional.

Box/open end wrenches: A 10mm wrench is most important. 8, 9 and 11mm wrenches are useful. Craftsman makes a set of very small, thin wrenches with a closed and open end on each wrench. Each wrench is a combination of sizes, i.e. 8+9 mm or 9+10 mm, so you can carry only two and have four sizes. These wrenches are cheap and light.

Pliers: We bring a Leatherman tool, which has pliers, knife, screwdrivers and more.

Patch kit: Be sure there are a variety of patch sizes, sandpaper, tire irons (2 minimum) and glue. (We carry more than one glue because once you open a glue, it can dry out.)

Spare tube: Be sure that the valve is correct (Presta or Schrader). Tubes also make a good sling if you hurt your arm.

Pump: Matter of preference.

Duct tape: We wrap about 16 inches of duct tape around the top of the seat post in case of emergencies. It comes in handy if you get a tire sidewall blow out. You can fix almost anything with duct tape!

Money - both paper and coin: Paper money is strong stuff. It can be used with duct tape to repair a tire sidewall blow out (see repair section). Bring coin money for phone calls.

Map or book: You need to know where you are going. If there are any doubts, be sure to bring a map or this book.

Emergency Repairs

Flat repair: If you have a new tube, put it in. If you only have a patch kit, repair the tube. Be sure to check the inside of the tire for thorns etc. If you have neither tube nor patch kit, be ready to try a few tricks. First, find the hole in the tube and mark it. Then tie off the tube so the hole is isolated. The tube is much smaller now but that's ok. Put one bead of the tire on the rim, then stretch the tube around the rim inside the tire. Use the tire irons and put the tire on. If that does not work it is time for Plan B. Leave the flat tube in the tire and stuff the tire full of grass, and we mean *stuff*, use a stick and pack it in.

Tire sidewall blowout: Take a dollar bill and rip or cut it to fit over the hole in the tire (much larger). Use the duct tape and fasten the bill to the inside of the tire. Fix flat tube if needed and you're off.

Broken chain: If you have a chain tool, use it to take out broken links. If not, try putting the chain back together and smash it together with two rocks.

Broken rear derailleur: If you have a chain tool, break the chain and remove the chain from the rear derailleur. Put the chain around the middle chain ring in the front and whatever rear cog lines up the straightest. Then crop the chain so there is no slack, and reattach. You won't be able to shift gears, but you will be able to ride out.

Broken spoke: Bend the broken spoke pieces around the other spokes so the wheel can spin freely. If you have a chain tool, tighten the two spokes (one on each side of the broken spoke) slightly.

Wheel taco (bent rim): Find the apex of the bend then give the wheel a swift whack against a solid object (i.e. tree or fencepost). Try to avoid rocks.

A2 Quick Tips to Improve Riding Skills

Here are some general mountain biking principles, riding techniques, and equipment that can improve your riding skills and increase your enjoyment.

General Biking Principles

There are two secrets to improved bike riding. First, watch better riders and second, practice. Here's what to look for.

Center of mass: Using your weight to control your center of mass is the key to maneuverability. If your butt is glued to the seat all the time, then the bike's center of mass is also stationary, which limits what the bike can do. Look at the best technical riders and you will see that their body is all over the place, relative to the position of the bike. For instance: When descending steep trails, keep your weight way back. When climbing, try to keep your weight over the rear wheel so it can dig in to the ground. When turning, put more weight on the outside pedal. When going over logs or rocks, roll your weight back, then up and forward.

Awareness: Watch the trail ahead of you and not your front wheel. The rule is "look down, go down." If you are watching your front tire hit the road, you will not see that big rock, root or dropoff coming and you will be unprepared. Keep your head up and focus on where you are going and how to get there. Anticipate, by picking a line 4-10' ahead of you and heading for it.

Shifting: Mountain bikes have lots of gears, use them! Active shifting allows you to have a smooth cadence (pedal stroke), which saves energy. Active shifting also allows you to stay seated on the bike, which helps you climb steep hills. Active shifting helps keep your speed up so you can maintain balance. However, just because your bike has the ability to be in 24 different gear combinations does not mean that you should use them all. Your bike chain should stay parallel to the frame as much as possible. Try not to be in the two smallest or two largest cogs at the same time (or even close to that). Your shifting will be poor and the chain will be put under undue stress.

Braking: Learn to regulate brake force and usage. Squeeze the brakes, don't grab them, even in an emergency. Remember that most of your braking power is in the front brake. If you wrench on it when you are in trouble, not only will you stop fast and go over the handle bars, but you will lose steering ability (if you manage to stay on). Brake only when needed; you have more control over the bike when the brakes are off. Brake before corners or turns, not when you are in them. When going down a rutted trail, don't brake while crossing the rut, it will cause the front tire to grab. A good rule is to use the smoothest and straightest parts of the trail to control speed and the rest of the trail for steering.

Crashing: If you want to get better at mountain biking, be ready to fall. Crashing is part of mountain biking, but getting hurt does not have to be. Learn how to fall down safely. Go to a park and practice crashing on the safety of grass.

Equipment

When your bike works smoothly and each part is doing its job, you can concentrate on riding. A clean bike and certain types of equipment can help accomplish this goal. Keeping your bike clean is easy, but picking good bike parts is not so easy. Most quality mountain bike parts are expensive and picking out the ones you really need can be confusing. For this reason, we have compiled a simple list of equipment preferences that can help move your concentration from the bike to the trail.

Clipless pedals: Clipless pedals and riding shoes (this is the type where you shoe clips into the pedal) are the key to staying on your bike. In rough conditions, they provide a way for you to have total control over your bike. Clipless pedals make the bike an extension of your body. They are at the very top of our recommendation list.

Front suspension: Front suspension helps keeps your tire in contact with the ground, which improves braking while on rough terrain. It also smoothes out the ride, which will help increase your vision and save your hands from getting sore.

Frames: All frames are not created equal. Pick one that fits your body and riding style. Frames that are too large restrict maneuverability, while frames that are too small lack stability and hinder climbing ability. Your body size is not the only factor. Pick a bike that fits your riding style. If you are a hammer head, or like tight, quick turning, get a frame with a steep head-tube angle (ask your local bike shop for details). If you crave downhill travel, pick a frame with a more relaxed head-tube angle.

Sun glasses: Sun glasses help keep you from tearing up (moist eyes) on the descents and getting poked in the eye. They also filter bright light so that your eyes can stay wide open and focused.

A3 History of Mountain Biking in Marin
by Joe Breeze

The First Fat Tire Bikes

Ever since the bicycle balloon tire was introduced in this country in the early 1930s, there have been people riding off-road on fat tires. These early riders rode one-speed bikes or may have cobbled together multi-speed bikes. Their efforts, however, came and went. They either weren't connected to the bicycle industry or were in an area or time with little hope of inspiring others to use and improve bicycles in this way. Those incidents remained isolated. It wasn't until the 1970s in Marin County, California, that a group of cyclists had the tenacity to develop their hobby into what would become a national, and later, world craze.

Author's Note

Mountain biking was invented in Marin County and Joe Breeze was one of the pioneers. Here is his personal account of the major events in Marin County that led to the modern mountain bike.

Putting the Mountain in Mountain Bikes

Mt. Tamalpais had for decades been host to many isolated incidences of off-road, balloon-tire use. One group of off-road cyclists, based in Larkspur, was known as the Canyon Gang. John York, Tom Slifka, Robert and Kim Kraft and their buddies even held untimed and often impromptu races on Mt. Tam as early as 1971.

In 1973, I and other members of the road-racing club Velo Club Tamalpais began showing up to our club meetings aboard stripped-down balloon-tire, one-speed bikes. Each of us had come across our ballooner in a different way, but we had all been influenced in some way by the Canyonites. We had discovered that the old ballooners were the ticket to exploring the dirt roads and trails of Mt. Tam and environs. Club member Marc Vendetti deserves credit for much of this. He had grown up in Larkspur where he had ridden with the Canyon Gang. His crossing over to road bikes and joining Velo Club Tam in 1974 was the catalyst for our ballooner mania. An important feature of these early bikes was their downhill worthiness. While road racing emphasized our muscular strength, ballooners gave us an outlet for displaying our bike-handling skills. The off-road frame of choice became the Schwinn Excelsior, which we found to have the best downhill handling traits and to be one of the most durable.

Adding Gears

According to Charlie Kelly, it wasn't until the summer of 1975 that anyone from the Marin group put a derailleur on an old ballooner. Gary Fisher cobbled together a five-speed Schwinn ballooner and his immediate hill-climbing prowess convinced others that multiple gearing was the way to go. Eventually he added a front derailleur and three chainrings in front, and drum brakes front and rear to improve braking. All these parts added to the heft of the bike, a multi-speed, mongrel-hybrid Excelsior weighed in at about 65 pounds. Over the next few years the bikes shed many pounds as riders substituted better and better parts from the road bike world. Fisher and others built up many of these bikes for friends and acquaintances.

Racing Down Repack

There was a bit of a rivalry among sub-groups situated in towns around the base of Mt. Tam, and since many of the riders were road racers, it was only natural that a race be held to prove who was the fastest off road. The first formal, timed race occurred October 21, 1976, on the east face of Pine Mountain, just north of Mt. Tam. The 2.1 mile, steeply pitched, 1300-foot downhill vaporized the old coaster brakes' grease into a contrail of smoke. Because competitors needed to repack their coaster brakes with grease after the race, the course was dubbed Repack.

Unknown Racer
Repack Race 1977

Charlie Kelly and Fred Wolf chose the course. Riders were sent off at two-minute intervals, the best riders going last to build excitement. Timing was by Navy chronometer and alarm clock. In all, 24 Repack races were held from 1976 to 1984. The fastest time of 4 minutes, 22 seconds was set by Gary Fisher. I had the most wins with ten, and the second fastest time of 4:24. The fastest woman was Wende Cragg at 5:27. Cragg was the first woman rider of the group, having started riding in 1975. Her fearless downhilling and unparalleled streak of riding off-road 75 days straight, left her the undisputed "Queen of Klunking" for many years. Cragg also shot many of the photos of the early days of the sport in Marin.

The First Breezers

Joe Breeze
First Breezer 1977

Repack was instrumental in bringing together all of Marin's ballooner sub-groups on a regular basis. By 1977, many Marin ballooners sported the finest and toughest road bike components from around the world. But all these parts were attached to the old Schwinn frames, which were strong only by virtue of their mass. In 1977, Charlie Kelly asked me to build him a new frame. I did, building ten frames of straight-gauge, chrome-moly airplane-frame tubing. I completed the first one in October 1977, and raced it to victory at Repack. It is considered the first successful purpose-built mountain bike frame. It was also the first ballooner built up using all-new parts. I finished the other nine bikes by June 1978. Called Breezers, they sold for $750 each, complete with pump, water bottle, spare tube and repair kit.

Up until that point, the old fat-tire bikes had been known, aside from ballooners, as clunkers, bombers, or beaters, owing to their rather ragged appearance. They had seen a lot of years, many in junkyards. The Breezers created quite a stir in the Marin bicycle community. Confirmed road cyclists who had been looking askance at their colleagues' ballooner riding, took a long look at the Breezer. Here was a shiny new,18-speed, 38-pound example of a fat-tire bike. Suddenly it became difficult to call fat-tire bikes "clunkers", and there came many new converts.

The Start of A National Trend

By the late '70s, the Marin mountain bike movement reached critical mass and word spread out of the county, across the country, and eventually around the world. The first national story about the phenomenon ran in the Spring 1978 edition of Co-Evolution Quarterly. Outside/Mariah magazine published a story by Charlie Kelly in 1979.

In January of 1979, I and my road-tandem partner (and ballooner buddy) Otis Guy went to visit fellow road-racer and framebuilder Tom Ritchey, who lived south of San Francisco. Ritchey had a very successful business making single and tandem road frames and had once been on the Junior National Cycling Team. When I wheeled my Breezer out of Otis's truck, Ritchey's eyes lit up. He exclaimed that he was planning to ride down the Sierra Nevada's John Muir Trail in the summer and the Breezer's balloon tires were the way to go.

Creating a Business

Gary Fisher, who had earlier chosen not to get a Breezer, was looking for someone to build him a fat-tire frame. Word got back to Fisher that Ritchey was interested in making such a frame and Fisher asked Ritchey to build him one. At Fisher's request, I sent my Breezer drawings to Ritchey. After delivering the finished frame, Ritchey built nine more frames and asked Gary Fisher if he would sell them in Marin. In September 1979, Fisher picked them up. Back in downtown Fairfax, he ran across his buddy Charlie Kelly. Showing him the gleaming frames, he asked Kelly if he would like to go into business with him to sell Ritchey's frames. They immediately pooled together their cash at hand (all $2000), opened a bank account, and came up with the business name MountainBikes. It was the first business established to sell nothing but fat-tire bikes. Fisher and Kelly, along with Ritchey, more than any others to date, showed a powerful commitment to the fledgling sport and got down to the business of getting fat-tire bikes into the hands of more people.

Ritchey had considerable frame-building experience, and was already showing a great deal of ingenuity in making road-racing bikes more mechanically efficient. Ritchey was able to deliver to MountainBikes quality fat-tire frames, forks, handlebar/stems, and bottom brackets on a timely basis, and business took off.

In 1980, Charlie Kelly started the first mountain bike-specific magazine. His Fat Tire Flyer was all alone in this field until 1985. Filled with event information, humorous anecdotes and even mountain bike comics, it reflected and amplified the growing enthusiasm for the sport.

The next step in the evolution was increased bike production. By 1981, a lot of people were plunking down $1400 for a Ritchey/MountainBike sold by Fisher and Kelly. In 1981, Mike Sinyard of Specialized Bicycle Imports bought a couple of Ritchey MountainBikes. His designer, Tim Neenan, suggested they do a Specialized mountain bike. Sinyard eventually took his Ritchey to their factory in Japan. This became the model for the first Specialized Stumpjumper, which made its debut in September 1981 at a bicycle trade show. With a price of $750 and wider availability, the bike made the sport accessible to more people. Thousands of Stumpjumpers were sold in the next two years.

From then on, every name in the bike business jumped into the fray. Mountain bike sales tripled every year for several years. By 1986, mountain bike sales surpassed road bike sales.

A4 Jurisdictions and Resources

Angel Island State Park

Facilities include Visitor Center, Museum, snack bar, picnic areas and camping. Fee for ferry. Bike on designated roads only.

Angel Island Park Headquarters 415-435-1915
Tiburon Ferry Information 415-435-2131

China Camp State Park

Facilities include Ranger Station, Museum, snack bar, picnic areas and camping. Parking fee for most areas. China Camp is unique among state parks in Marin because bikes are allowed on most single track.

China Camp Park Headquarters 415-456-0766

Golden Gate National Recreation Area (GGNRA)

Facilities include Visitor Center, historic forts, Marine Mammal Center, picnic areas and camping. Bike on designated roads only.

Marin Headlands Visitor Center 415-331-1540
Stinson Beach Weather Info 415-868-1922

Speed Limits!

In general, the maximum bike speed is 15 mph on all public lands in Marin. Slow to 5 mph when approaching curves or when passing others. If necessary, bikers should yield to hikers and horses.

Marin County Open Space District (MCOSD)

No facilities. Bikes are allowed on all fire roads.

Marin County Open Space District Office 415-499-6387

Marin Municipal Water District (MMWD)

Facilities include Ranger Station and picnic area. No swimming. Entrance fee for cars in main lakes area. Bikes allowed on all fire roads except where prohibited by signs.

Sky Oaks Ranger Station 415-459-5267

Mt. Tamalpais State Park

Facilities include Ranger Station, Museum, outdoor theater, snack bar, picnic areas and camping. Parking fee for some areas. Bike on designated roads only.

Pantoll Ranger Station and Campground 415-388-2070

Point Reyes National Seashore (PRNS)

Facilities include three Visitor Centers, gift shop and snack bar. Bike on designated roads only.

Bear Valley Visitor Center 415-663-1092.
Lighthouse Weather Info 415-663-9029

Samuel P. Taylor State Park

Facilities include Ranger Station, picnic areas and camping. Entrance fee to main area. Bike on designated roads only.

Samuel P. Taylor Park Headquarters 415-488-9897

Bicycle Trails Council of Marin

The Bicycle Trails Council of Marin was formed in 1987 to promote safe, responsible mountain biking. The BTC is dedicated to the acceptance of mountain biking as a legitimate and environmentally sound recreational use of the land. The BTC works to educate bikers, as well as other users of local regulations and proper trail etiquette.

The BTC serves as an advocate for the mountain biking community. The BTC organizes and directs efforts by mountain bikers to become involved in the conservation, administration and maintenance of the public lands of Marln. The BTC meets with the various land agencies and is politically active in supporting the belief that mountain bikers should be treated as equal members of the outdoor user community.

The BTC is an all volunteer organization that depends entirely upon the involvement of its members.

Phone: 415-456-7512
Address: PO Box 494, Fairfax 94978
Web Page: www.btcmarin.org

Wombats - Women's Mountain Bike And Tea Society

The WOMBAT mission is to sustain a women's off-road cycling network so that members may find a riding partner; encourage girls and women to try cycling for the fun of it; learn the trails in their area; improve their riding skills; keep up with the latest news of interest on "women who love mud too much"; enhance awareness of bicycles as a mode of transportation; in short, change the world.

Address: PO Box 757 Fairfax CA 94978
Web Page: www.wombats.org

Marin County Bicycle Coalition

Address: PO Box 35, San Anselmo, CA 94979
Web page: www.bikadelic.com

A5 Map Index

This index lists map entries only. Numbers refer to ride numbers.

Trails and Roads - If the ride number is bold text, then the ride uses that trail. If the ride number is plain text, then the trail appears on the map, but is not part of the ride.

Place Names, Mountains and Lakes - These are included in the index if they are on the map and the ride comes near the area.

Index Continued

A6 About the Authors

Theresa Martin grew up in Marin County, attending Drake High School and the College of Marin. She has Masters degrees in Biology and Exercise Physiology and is currently a Biology Professor at San Mateo Community College. She has been riding mountain bikes in Marin since 1984.

Brian Simon also grew up in Marin County, attending Drake High, the College of Marin and UC Berkeley. He has raced mountain bikes professionally and is currently working in the computer industry on the peninsula.

Don Martin is a retired Physics teacher from the College of Marin. He and his wife have written and published three hiking books. He developed his map-making skills while working on the hiking books.

Book Ordering Information

Books available from Martin Press:

Mountain Biking Marin
40 Great Rides in Marin County
Theresa Martin and Brian Simon
© 1998
112 Pages, $10.95

Hiking Marin
121 Great Hikes in Marin County
Don and Kay Martin
© 1995
304 Pages, $18.95

MT TAM
A Hiking, Running and Nature Guide
Don and Kay Martin
2nd edition, © 1994
128 Pages, $9.95

Point Reyes National Seashore
A Hiking and Nature Guide
Don and Kay Martin
2nd edition, © 1997
136 Pages, $9.95

All four books may be ordered from your local bookstore or directly from the publisher at the address below.
Please include $3.00 per book to cover shipping and tax.

Martin Press
P.O. Box 2109
San Anselmo, CA 94979
www.marintrails.com